D1356407

A CANDLE WAS LIT

A CANDLE WAS LIT

LIFE OF MOTHER MARY AIKENHEAD

By

MARGERY BAYLEY BUTLER

"There is not enough darkness in all the world to put out the light of one small candle"

DUBLIN
CLONMORE AND REYNOLDS LTD.

LONDON
BURNS OATES AND WASHBOURNE LTD.

First Published 1953
Reprinted 1954.

NIHIL OBSTAT: M. L. DEMPSEY, S.T.D.
CENSOR THEOL. DEP.
IMPRIMI POTEST: ✠IOANNES CAROLUS
ARCHIEP. DUBLINEN
HIBERNIÆ PRIMAS
11 MAY, 1953

MADE AND PRINTED IN THE
REPUBLIC OF IRELAND BY
CAHILL AND CO., LTD., FOR
CLONMORE AND REYNOLDS LTD.

Contents

List of Illustrations

Cover design and drawings by Pauline Hayes.

Introduction

Mary Aikenhead was born on January 19th, 1787. The date is significant in several ways. For Irish Catholics the burthen of life had eased considerably, since the fury of persecution had spent itself without decisive result. In Dublin Castle and beyond the sea, in Westminster, ministers and their officials had accepted as obvious the fact that the Irish people could not be deprived of the Catholic Faith by force. A "Catholic Committee" had been formed some thirty years before and though its timidity was proverbial, its very existence was a proof that the worst of the Penal Days was over. Many of the painful restraints imposed upon Catholics were removed by the Relief Bills of 1778 and 1782. By the Act of the year last mentioned they were allowed to live in the cities of Cork and Galway. They were still excluded from political life and public offices, from the army and from the legal profession, but they were allowed to practise medicine and to purchase, inherit and bequeath property. From the status of a slave the Catholic had risen to be half a citizen.

Legislative independence came to Ireland in 1782. As the legislators were all Protestant, intent on maintaining their own ascendancy, the concession of further reliefs to the huge Catholic majority was bitterly resisted. Thanks, however, to pressure from Pitt, who feared to have a dangerously discontented Ireland on his flank in the approaching war with the French republic, Catholics were given, in 1793, the parliamentary franchise, though they were not allowed to enter Parliament themselves. They were permitted also to become magistrates, simple barristers, officers in the army and navy. More important, perhaps, to them as a body, was the stimulus which Grattan's Parliament gave to Irish trade. Merchants, like John Keogh and Edward Byrne, leaders of the Catholic Committee in Dublin, were wealthy men, as were many of their kind in Cork, Limerick, Waterford and the other towns. Still better endowed with worldly goods was the Protestant society in Cork to which Mary Aikenhead belonged as a growing girl.

But there was another, inexpressibly sad side to this picture of material progress. The condition of the poor belied the hopes of Grattan and his friends, for it did not improve, and by the end of the century was extremely low. In 1796 it could be written of Dublin: "The east part of the capital displays some grandeur in palaces, public buildings and works which, instead of disguising, rather make more glaring, the huge poverty, the gigantic misery that fills this great city, in every garb, in every shape of human woes and gradation of wretchedness, from those who excite gentle compassion to those that petrify with horror; every street and lane, every place of public resort are crowded with squalid victims of oppression, while in the silent recesses of bashful woe, famine, nakedness and their concomitant distresses claim their thousands." Worse still was the condition of the rural countryside: "wherever we turn our eyes, we are everywhere stared in the face by the poverty, the nakedness, the miserable filthy styes of a distressed, woe-worn peasantry."

For this unhappy state of affairs there were many causes. The war with France had driven up prices. Between 1782 and 1803 the population increased from an estimated 3,000,000 to 5,000,000, without any corresponding addition to the country's resources. So burning was the passion for land that rents were paid on a scale which left nothing beyond bare subsistence to the tillers of the soil. Thus arose for an enormous proportion of the people of Ireland a number of chronic evils—the lowest standards of living, debt, disease, premature death. Mary Aikenhead in her teens saw sights that must have brought grievous pain to her tender heart. It was these experiences, no doubt, which influenced her decision, once she had grown to womanhood, to devote her life to the service of the poor and suffering.

During the forty-three years spent by her as a nun the economic condition of the country continued to be deplorable. It is a commonplace of history that in the first half of the 19th century the state of those who lived by agriculture in Ireland—and in 1844 they were calculated to be 66 per cent. of the population—was miserable in the extreme. Their privations and hardships were a byword in Europe and America. Things became even worse in 1846, when the Corn Laws were repealed and the preference given to Irish farm products—in virtue of which Ireland had been transformed into an agricultural and tillage country—suddenly removed. The upset to the whole economy of the nation can easily be imagined. When agriculture thereby became a desperately depressed industry the only remedies found were eviction, emigration and famine. Gladstone's first Land Act, which afforded the tenant some protection in his dealings with the landlord, came as late as 1870.

In industries other than agriculture there was similar decay and distress. Theoretically they were placed on the same footing as those of England by the Act of Union; in practice they could not withstand the unrestrained competition of the latter, which had been skilfully developed, fostered and encouraged for centuries. By 1825 it was obvious that the Union had destroyed all the weak and struggling manufacturing industries of the country. This hit the merchant class, to which many Catholics belonged, in the cities of Dublin, Cork, Limerick and Waterford and in the towns. Dublin became a dead capital, and its fall in prosperity affected the rest of Ireland. Add to these misfortunes high imperial and local taxes, tithes, tolls and absentee landlords, who spent their rents abroad, and it will be clear that during the whole lifetime of Mary Aikenhead poverty in Ireland, both in town and country, was on a stupendous scale.

The purpose of this book is to show what one holy and capable woman did to soothe the sorrows and lessen the burthens of Ireland's poor. She was one of the many engaged in that noble work. If the light shed by each candle was small the light from all together did reach into the darkest corners and do much to dispel the prevailing gloom. Dublin was at this epoch remarkable for the extent of its charities supported by voluntary contributions. Mary's great friend, Mrs. O'Brien, a woman of the world, though a most unworldly woman, was a worthy precursor of those of her sex who in later times have been zealous associate members of St. Vincent de Paul conferences, Children of Mary sodalities, Legion of Mary præsidia. She was fortunate in enjoying the sympathy and support of Most Reverend Dr. Murray, the apostolic archbishop whose kindliness, energy, patience, prudence, supernatural charm wrought wonders of restoration in Dublin and throughout his diocese. And she was fortunate, too, in her daughters, young girls, for the most part, from the Catholic homes of Ireland, whose talent and virtue proved equal to every task.

The service of the poor, as Mary Aikenhead understood it, was exacting. Her Sisters of Charity were soon a familiar sight in the festering slums. When cholera ravaged Dublin and Cork in 1832, the Sisters moved like ministering angels among the stricken. They established free schools. They cared for orphans, and the time would come when they would provide homes, too, for the aged and the blind. They established industries that workers might be able to keep themselves in reasonable comfort by their own honest toil. Day by day they visited the sick, the afflicted, the destitute, bearing gifts of medicine, food and clothing for the body, bringing consolation to the soul. St. Mary Magdalen's Asylum was built in Donnybrook for rescue work. A missionary centre that was later to become a hospice for the dying was opened at Harold's Cross. Mother Aikenhead had even the courage to found, equip and manage St. Vincent's Hospital, the first Catholic hospital in Dublin, and to start it on a career of distinction to which every generation since has added lustre. And when the number of her daughters grew, she sent out colonies to England and Australia.

These activities, all physically wearing and some repugnant to the refined nature of woman, demanded great generosity and readiness for sacrifice in the Sisters. She made sure then to give them a thorough grounding in the fundamental principles of asceticism. St. Ignatius was chosen as the model. The institute which she bequeathed to her followers was based on the Rules and Constitutions of the Society of Jesus. *Caritas Christi urget nos*: in service to the poor and afflicted they were to show their love for Christ, the Eternal King. More important than the written word was her own example. Practical, as became a lady of solid Scot ancestry, full of good sense, almost masculine in the breadth and power of her understanding, direct to the borders of brusqueness, she was nevertheless genial, good-natured, simple and humorous in her dealings with others. For twenty-seven years, till released by death in 1858, she was the victim of ill-health. Perhaps her chief spiritual characteristics were an intense spirit of faith, showing itself in absolute conformity with God's will and utter trust in God's Providence. All through her religious life her dearest wish had been to remain unknown, as far as the duties of her office permitted. But the intensity of her love for Christ, from which her works of charity sprang, could not easily be concealed. Outside and inside the Congregation stories were told and retold, among those who knew her well, of her nobility and virtues. Pressure of work in all the houses led to delay in committing this evidence to paper. But the tradition of her holiness was so strong that the question of her beatification could not permanently be shelved. It was no surprise, therefore, when competent ecclesiastical authorities in Dublin took the matter in hand and after the proper steps had been taken sent on their report to Rome. On March 15th, 1921, the Decree for the introduction of the Cause of her Beatification was signed by Pope Benedict XV. What joy there will be in Ireland and beyond if one day this great Lover of the Poor is raised to the honours of the altar!

JOHN RYAN, S.J.

6th February, 1953.

In expressing my gratitude to all those who have assisted me I must mention the following as deserving of special thanks: Father James Brodrick, S.J., whose sympathetic judgement in the beginning helped me to persevere; Father John Ryan, S.J., for his constant help, judicious criticism and unwearied patience; my sister Beatrice and her husband, Mr. Frederick E. Dixon, for their competent advice at all stages and generosity in undertaking to do the proof reading; Miss Joan Dempsey for her excellent typescript; and lastly, the Congregation of the Irish Sisters of Charity at home and in Australia for the support of their kindly interest, their approval and their prayers.

In addition, I must acknowledge the considerable use made of the earlier life of Mother Mary Aikenhead by Mrs. Sarah Atkinson, which includes practically all the authentic information available, and which has necessarily been used as a basis for much of the present work.

M.B.B.

March, 1953.

CHAPTER I

The Age of Innocence

"DAVID!"

"Come in, little woman, and welcome!"

There was surprise in his voice as, rising from a table littered with books and papers, and holding out both hands to her, he drew his wife gently to the sofa and seated himself beside her.

"To what do I owe this visit?" he went on; and then in a tone of mock alarm, "you're not coming to tell me I must submit to having my 'study' spring-cleaned—at long last?" He looked as he spoke around his small domain, which would have filled any feminine heart with despair. It was a typical student's room—books lined the walls, covered table and desk and overflowed on to the floor, together with hundreds of pamphlets, papers, letters, and woe betide the hand that dared disturb their resting-place! It was only under severe protest that sweeping or dusting operations were ever performed, while any partial improvement was not infrequently followed by confusion worse than ever, as the exasperated doctor searched frantically for some precious document mislaid by over-tidy female fingers—while his laments filled the guilty ears of wife and servant. Truly, it was no place for a woman, and Mrs. Aikenhead, a perfect housekeeper, normally gave her husband's study a wide berth; yet, here she was, on a late June evening in the year 1787, her gay pink dress making a welcome splash of colour against the sombre background.

Her husband's eyes lingered on the pale oval of her face framed by clusters of light-brown curls, but in the blue eyes which looked up into his, there was no answering smile as she said rather falteringly: "I—I'm worried about Mary."

"No need, my dear," reassured the doctor soothingly. "She's a fragile little creature, but organically sound."

"But I don't believe she's thriving. Kathleen Roche and Ellen

O'Regan were here to-day and they said for her age our Mary should be——"

"Yes, yes, I know," he interrupted. "You spent the afternoon comparing babies, and—" with a twinkle in his eye, "your dainty little nose is out of joint."

"No, it isn't," she said quietly, "and if that's all you've got to say——" Then as a faint cry came from the room above: "She's awake now, I must go to her."

Her head erect, one hand holding up her flounced skirt, she departed, injured dignity in every line of her trim figure.

"Out of joint," she murmured to herself, ascending the stairs leading to the nursery, "out of joint, indeed! Heartless, that's what he is, just like all men," and then with womanly inconsistency, she added: "He's the best man in the world."

A slight noise behind her made her turn round. Deep in her thoughts, she had not realised that her husband had followed her and was just behind her on the staircase; head bowed, hands clasped before him, he was a picture of abject contrition.

"My Lady Fair," he murmured, "a thousand apologies, 'tip-tilted,' I should have said. 'Tis the prettiest nose on the prettiest face on earth——"

"For goodness' sake have sense," she smiled, in spite of her anxiety. "Surely you didn't really think I was offended?" And hand in hand the young couple entered the nursery and stood looking down at the cot where their treasured little daughter lay, emitting inarticulate coos and gurgles.

"Now, Doctor David, as a professional man, what do you think of her?"

"Now, Mrs. Aikenhead, as mother of this delightful child, what do *you wish* me to think?"

"That she's far too pale and thin, and that a change of air is what she needs," came the swift reply. "Mrs. Rorke would be only too delighted to take her and——"

"Oho! So that's the idea, is it?" smiled the doctor. "You have already prescribed the treatment and you only want me to agree, my wily madam. Well, who is this Mrs. Rorke?"

"She's a very respectable person who lives just beyond the city—you've had patients on Eason's Hill, haven't you? Her cottage is midway up, and she tells me the air is particularly fresh on that side of Cork. Her husband is a labourer, a hard-working, honest man."

"Papists, I suppose?" the doctor arched an eyebrow.

"Well, ye-es," came the slow reply, and then, more quickly, "just like me."

"But you're not superstitiously so." She made no response. "However, my darling," he went on, "if it will ease your mind, get your Mrs. Rorke up some afternoon and we'll see what can be done. It isn't everyone to whom we could hand over our lovely little girl."

* * * * * *

A week or so later the doctor's smart carriage and pair drove up Eason's Hill, causing quite a disturbance amongst the denizens of that neighbourhood. Eyes peeped from behind curtains; heads popped over half-doors; while the smaller fry, dropping apparently from out of the blue, stood agape on the roadside, surveying the unusual sight.

With a "whoa!" from Paddy, a crunching of hooves and a jingling of harness, the carriage came to a stop outside the Rorkes' tidy little cottage. Mrs. Rorke, a comfortable body, apple-cheeked, middle-aged, stood at the garden gate, ready to welcome her honoured visitors. 'Twas many a long day since such a grand pair had appeared on Eason's Hill. She proudly ushered them up the path, through the pretty little garden where, to her boundless delight, Dr. Aikenhead admired her John's roses.

"You'll take good care of her for us, won't you?" asked Mrs. Aikenhead, smiling trustfully into the other woman's pleasant, homely face.

"Indeed, ma'am, you may depend on me," was the reply. "Sure, haven't I reared five of me own," and taking the precious bundle into her well-practised arms, "she'll be as right as rain with Mammy Rorke, ye need have no fear—God bless us, God bless us"—as the baby yawned and sneezed. "Isn't she the darlin' little lamb!"

"Well, Mrs. Rorke, she's in your charge now," boomed the deep voice of the doctor, "and if there's anything you need, you know where to send——"

"Thank you kindly, sir, and you, too, my lady," said she, bobbing a curtsey. "May the blessing of God be with ye both," as they moved towards the door, the doctor bending his head to avoid hitting the lintel.

" We wish you the same," he replied. " Come, my dear," and he escorted his wife down the path, bordered by diminutive flower beds, to the carriage where Paddy, aware of their coming, was cracking his whip fearsomely and growling, " Be off wid ye," to the swarming crowd of children.

At the cottage door Mrs. Rorke stood with Mary in her arms watching their departure. She noted how gallantly the doctor helped his wife in, then paused to raise his hat and bow in her direction. " As if I had blue blood meself," she said later, while Mrs. Aikenhead smiled tremulously from the carriage window and waved kisses to her baby. The next instant, with a final crack of the whip and a subdued cheer from the lads, the carriage bowled away down the hill, rounded the corner and disappeared from view.

" Isn't it the fine pair they make?" thought Mrs. Rorke, as she turned from the door. " Och, 'tis a thousand pities about himself—a grand man like him—so good to the poor an' all. God forgive *her,* that's all I say, she has a lot to answer for, dear, dear, dear," and shaking her head over Mrs. Aikenhead's defections, she placed the baby in the cradle and bustled about the spotless kitchen to have the tea ready for John's return.

That night she saw the nearest thing to a soirée ever held on Eason's Hill. From far and near, neighbours and friends gathered, all agog to gaze on Dr. Aikenhead's little girl, and many were the sympathetic tongues that were clucked over her, the general opinion being that the change of air would make her " come on wonderful."

After the first excitement of the baby's arrival had died away, life on the Hill went on just as usual. From the start she had settled down quite contentedly, and as the days grew to weeks and the weeks to months, all signs of her earlier delicacy vanished, and except for her pretty clothes and refined appearance, no one, seeing her in the company of the other cottage children, would have taken her to be anything but one of themselves.

Mrs. Rorke watched over every phase of her development with a proud and jealous eye—dare anyone say a word against her darling! Yet there was no petting or spoiling. Mary was taught to stand on her own two feet and to fight her own childish battles. While, if her young charge gave trouble or showed the least sign of obstinacy, punishment followed the offence as surely as night follows the day. Mary was three years old before she learnt to speak, but after that—

MOTHER MARY AIKENHEAD

A Nun in the making

womanlike—her tongue never ceased to chatter. The whole world around her was a source of wonder; she herself, a perpetual note of interrogation.

Happy as they were together, there was one cloud on Mammy Rorke's mind; she was weighed down with the burden of a secret which she knew could not always remain hidden.

"Truth will out," she often said to herself. "May God and His Blessed Mother give me the grace to speak."

Having kept her secret to herself for nearly three years, she could stand it no longer, so one fine day, leaving Mary in the care of a neighbour, off she went into Cork and up the Parade to the doctor's house. There she confessed to Mrs. Aikenhead that she had had her child baptised a Catholic. . . .

Curious eyes had noted her departure in the morning; still more curious ones watched for her return; there was a veritable battery of them focussed on her as she journeyed up the Hill, tired but elated, and an unusual number of women looked over their half-doors to bid her good evening as she passed—but their unspoken questions were ever to remain unanswered.

Life on Eason's Hill was full of absorbing interest for an intelligent child like Mary. There was always something new to be seen and wondered at, fluffy yellow chicks cuddling into their proud mother hen, a playful kitten brought to the cottage as a gift, baby pigs with curly tails, grunting and squealing in the sty, or maybe a jar full of tiddlers, the catch of a juvenile fisherman in some nearby stream. Flowers, too, she loved, and she would watch Daddy John Rorke by the hour as he worked in the tiny garden; sometimes sowing seeds with her own wee fingers, or helping to give a drink to thirsty plants.

Amongst the Hill children she was in her element: Nuala, Dessie, Timmy, Sheila, Rory with the crooked back, and the rest, and if she loved them they certainly loved her in return. She had many older friends, too; there was Biddy who travelled the roads with her wares: ribbons, combs, laces, rings, brooches, beads and buckles. "Biddy the Hawker" was her official title. Then there was "Tommy the Tinman," who could mend a saucepan while you waited; Joanie, whose chief source of income was the sale of sprats; and last and dearest to her heart, came Sean.

Sean would have exercised a breathless fascination over any little girl, and especially over one who was always clad in the whitest of frilly dresses, and whose face, neck, hands—whose whole person—was subjected to a merciless scrubbing at the least suspicion of dirt. For Sean was black, a delightful dirty black that came off on to one's fingers and could be transferred to face and dress, that is, if one were fortunate enough to escape Mammy's vigilant eye, and get within touching distance of him.

He was an elderly man who spent his days working as a coal porter on the Quay, and his evenings amongst the young folk on the Hill. A born story-teller, he knew how to keep his audience in suspense right to the last minute, and await with a chuckle their " oh's " and " ah's " of astonishment at some unexpected dénouement. Fairies, goblins, leprechauns all came to life at his voice, and what was more, his stories were true, you could take his word for it, and when Mary, endeavouring to arouse Mammy Rorke's interest in a crock of gold found only last week under a bush in Youghal, would assert firmly: " But he said so, Mammy. He said he knew a man whose cousin bought a house with the money," Mrs. Rorke would only smile and say: " All right, my love, but many's the time I was in Youghal meself and never heard tale nor tidings of the like."

Occasionally her pleasures took a more sophisticated form—a trip to the city to her parents' house, followed by a walk on the Parade, the promenade of fashion in Cork, where her chestnut curls and large expressive dark grey eyes, her childish gaiety, her frank and sometimes disconcerting remarks on everything she saw, were bound to attract attention. But from the day she demanded: " Take me down the Parade again, me know me are a pretty child," their outings in this direction were no more. Mrs. Rorke wasn't going to have her darling's head turned by foolish compliments, while any further attempts at looking for notice on the part of her young charge were dealt with just as summarily.

Sunday was the day of days on Eason's Hill, when the entire population, old and young, went to Mass in the Bishop's Chapel. Mary, as a matter of course, went too, sometimes skipping alongside Mammy Rorke, or perched on Daddy John's shoulder, from where she had an uninterrupted view of all that went on around them, the narrow road thronged with people, old grannies in their hooded cloaks, younger women with frilly white bonnets, men with gaily coloured waistcoats and flowing cravats, barefooted children running here and there in everybody's way. The chapel was far too small to hold the congregation, many of whom had to be content with kneeling in the yard, but Daddy John always secured front seats for his "family" where they could hear and see everything.

As the priest came out from the sacristy an expectant hush fell on the crowd of worshippers, broken only by the gentle rattle of well-worn beads, the scrape of feet, the tinkle of the bell and, at the most solemn part, a groan of fervour or a thumping of a nearby breast reached the ears of the little girl, who was busily trying to remember all that Mammy had told her about the Holy Mass and what she was to say to dear Jesus, the "Little Son of God" when He came down on the altar.

Strangely enough, Dr. Aikenhead made no objection to his daughter's attendance at chapel. Frequently his carriage passed them on the road as he drove in state to the morning service at Shandon Church. Once he stopped and invited Mary to step in and go along with him, but when the little girl hid behind Mammy Rorke's cloak and cried vigorously:

"No, no, me go to Mass with Mammy," he only laughed indulgently and said:

"Go, child, go," thinking meanwhile to himself that once she left Eason's Hill, all that would be forgotten.

But if Sunday was the best day of the week, just before bedtime was the best hour of the day, when gathered together in the cosy kitchen, the firelight shining on the well-polished pots and pans and dancing on the walls, Daddy, Mammy and little "Miss Mary" knelt down to say the Rosary. Mammy Rorke shared her beads with Mary, who loved to hold on to the large crucifix, now and again pressing her lips affectionately to the places "where the nails hurt poor Jesus" or to "the thorns that made His head so sore." Sometimes before the numerous trimmings were half over, her own little head would start nodding, eyelids heavy with sleep, and by the time the last Hail Mary was said she would be away in the land of dreams, curled up like a little kitten on Mammy's shawl.

CHAPTER II

Her Father's House

"TIME TO get up, Miss Mary. Wake up, Alanna, or you'll be late for school."

Mary's only reply was to snuggle down deeper into the bed-clothes and pretend she hadn't heard.

"Miss Mary," Mammy's voice was peremptory now, and held a warning note that had never yet failed to take effect, "if you don't get up this instant I'll——"

There was no need to say more, for with a supreme effort the little girl jumped out of bed and stood on the floor, blinking sleepily at her new surroundings. Instead of being in the tiny white-washed, low-ceilinged bedroom of the cottage on Eason's Hill, she found herself in the middle of a large and airy nursery whose creamy wallpaper was liberally decorated with roses, ranging in colour from palest pink to deepest red, and through whose open windows floated the sound of a city already astir. Tripping over her long white nightgown the little girl ran to look. In the street below preparations for another day's work were already afoot; men passed up and down, bound for their various places of employment—clerks, clad in sober black, en route for the warehouses and shipping offices; labourers with their tools clumping along in heavy boots; gentlemen riding on horseback followed at a discreet distance by their grooms; while directly underneath her window, as well as farther up the street, apprentices with "shining morning faces" were busily, and with a great deal of laughter and rattling of chains, removing the shutters from the shop-fronts. The rising sun was rapidly dispelling the morning mist and revealing innumerable chimney pots and roof-tops interspersed with graceful spires and steeples. In the distance, here and there between the houses, she could catch a glimpse of the River Lee, whose "pleasant waters" and tree-covered banks lent an added air of beauty to the city.

Dr. Aikenhead has been so pleased with the progress of his little daughter and with the care taken of her on Eason's Hill that he had allowed her to remain there till she was six years old. When he had finally decided to bring her back to the city, he asked Mrs. Rorke to come too and take over the reins in the nursery, where Mary's younger sisters, Anne and Margaret, would benefit by her training. It had not been difficult to find a position for John as well in the busy household. The doctor was also an apothecary, and on the ground floor of their house he had a large and up-to-date establishment, trading under the title of Aikenhead and Dupont, whose prescriptions were so " accurately compounded " that it had a high reputation amongst the citizens and medical men of the place.

Not only was he esteemed, and rightly so, in his professional capacity, but was also greatly respected socially. Of Scottish Protestant descent, he had gradually come to love the land of his adoption. All his sympathies were with her people, and he entered into the plans and shared the hopes of many of the United Irishmen. Some of these were of Cork origin themselves, like the Emmets and John and Henry Sheares, whose father was a banker in Patrick Street. Once when Lord Edward Fitzgerald, in the guise of a Quaker, took shelter in his house, the doctor, hearing that the sheriff and his troops were in the offing, aided him to escape, and later had his house raided. Luckily for him, nothing came to light. The incriminating documents remained safely in their hiding-place, an innocent-looking drawer in the shop, filled with medical prescriptions.

He was a man of strong religious principles. Perhaps the only time he ever deviated from these was when he married a " dangerous Papist," gentle Mary Stackpole, the eldest daughter of a Catholic merchant. It was as a sop to conscience that he insisted that all the children of the marriage should be brought up Protestants. Much though he loved his wife and respected her views, he had the social position of his future family to consider, for in those days to be Protestant was synonymous with being respectable.

Now that his eldest child was the picture of health, as her rosy cheeks and firm young limbs proclaimed, he arranged for her to attend a nearby school, established for the purpose of educating the daughters of Protestant gentlemen, where she was instructed in the three R's and other accomplishments, French, embroidery, music, dancing, knowledge of which was deemed essential to a young lady who would one day take her place in Society.

So Mary spent her mornings at school where, besides the aforementioned subjects, great stress was laid on dignity and decorum. She was taught to sit, stand and walk correctly, a book balanced on her head; to curtsey and say: "Yes, thank you, ma'am," or "No, thank you, ma'am" when spoken to by her elders; in short, to exhibit all the signs of what was considered good breeding.

However, school didn't last all day, and in the afternoons she was comparatively free—free to peep into the shop where, if business happened to be slack, a friendly apprentice would show her the bottles of medicine with their beautiful colours or shake a drop of perfume on to her handkerchief—a risky business, for Mammy Rorke had a keen sense of smell—or even prescribe a powder for a sick dolly, to be administered later on under conditions of the utmost secrecy.

Usually in the afternoons Mammy took her three little charges for a walk, Anne and Margaret held firmly by either hand. Mary, allowed greater latitude, was permitted to run about here and there, meeting any of her school friends who also happened to be taking the air accompanied by their Nannies. Patrick Street and the South Mall were their favourite objectives. One could stand by the hour gazing into the attractively dressed windows of the fine shops, or better still, one could watch the boats coming up to the landing place and see the men unloading them—cask after cask being hauled up with ropes from the innermost depths of the vessel and then rolled down the gangway on to the Quay and away to the stores on the ground floor of the merchants' houses.

One market day, when the usual walk had to be foregone owing to the crowded streets, Mammy Rorke and the little girls stood in the shelter of a neighbouring shop door and from their point of vantage surveyed the scene in comparative safety. All was wild confusion—droves of cattle with their shouting owners; cars rattled recklessly over the cobbles; pigs grunted here and there, nosing their way along the gutters in search of tit-bits; while the cackling of hens, the cries of those making bargains, the cheers when the bargains were clinched added to the general uproar. Further along the street small booths were erected where one bought almost anything from Peggy's Leg to pins and needles. Mary's quick eye was not long in picking out one particular booth where a white-haired old woman was selling ribbons, lace and other similar odds and ends. Before Mrs. Rorke was aware of what was happening, with a wild cry of "Biddy, Biddy!" she slipped away and off up the street with her in between cows and bullocks, under horses' heads, past the grunting pigs, on, on she ran, while Mammy alternated between fear for her darling's safety and shame at her utter lack of dignity and decorum, "an' her a doctor's daughter!" Little Anne and Margaret, lifting up their childish voices, wept long and loudly for their beloved sister.

Meanwhile, Mary, with a cry of joy, hurled herself into the old woman's arms, her chestnut curls flying ribbonless, her dainty shoes destroyed—one can imagine the condition of the street—but she didn't care, at the moment that is, the black day of reckoning was to come later! After she'd been hugged and kissed and presented with a new hair ribbon, she allowed herself to be led back by a kindly farmer to Mrs. Rorke, who greeted her frigidly with a "wait-till-your-father-hears-this" look in her eye, but Anne and Margaret received her with open arms. Suffice it to say that Patrick Street on market day was out of bounds for evermore.

Later on, as Mary grew tall and sensible, and as the nursery quarters were becoming crowded owing to the addition of a baby brother, St. John, she was promoted to the society of her elders and took her meals in state with her parents and any guests who happened to be enjoying their hospitality. As her family of dolls accompanied her and had their own special corner of the drawing-room, Mary's visits to the nursery gradually grew rarer, especially as she had also her own little bedroom.

Mrs. Rorke dreaded what would happen next. She knew it was bound to come; already the doctor himself was superintending Miss Mary's night prayers and had expressed his displeasure at her "crossing herself" and "praying to the Virgin." At last the blow fell.

One Saturday evening when dinner was just over, Dr. Aikenhead looked across the table at his young daughter and said quietly:

"Mary will come to church with me to-morrow."

"Oh, Papa!" she cried delightedly, slipping off her chair and running to him, "how lovely!" Mrs. Aikenhead drew in her breath quickly, her cheeks grew even paler.

"O my God," she thought, "is there nothing I can do, is there no way out of it?"

There was only one way and she knew it, yet dared not take it. The only time she had ever opposed her husband's wishes was when she had contrived to get Mary out to Eason's Hill. A born pacifist, her policy in life was a smiling acquiescence, a gentle taking of the line of least resistance.

If the doctor noticed her sudden silence, he gave no sign, while Mary chattered excitedly till it was time for her to go to bed.

The next morning as the famous Bells of Shandon were pealing over the city and surrounding countryside, Dr. and Miss Aikenhead drove sedately in their carriage through practically deserted streets. Now and again he cast sidelong glances at her, the glances of a proud and loving father. She wore a flounced white dress gathered at the waist by a pale blue silk sash. Her cloak, hood and little shoes were of the same delicate shade, while from her wrist dangled a miniature reticule, the replica of one her mama had, embroidered with tiny pink flowers. Her little mittened hands clasped her father's latest gift to her, a tastefully bound Book of Common Prayer.

As they drew near the church, the street became crowded, carriages and sedan chairs bound for Shandon, humbler folk on foot, bound for the Bishop's Chapel. Mary got so excited greeting her old friends from Eason's Hill and there was so much blowing of kisses and waving of handkerchiefs that the good doctor had to say at last:

" Restrain yourself, my child," and then as, unheeding, she leaned out of the carriage calling: " Sean, Sean,"

" And who may I ask is Sean?"

" Oh! Papa," she replied, delighted to get a chance of doing her old friend a good turn, " Sean is the man you must get your coals from the next time you want any."

When at length they reached Shandon and joined the crowd of elegantly attired gentlemen and beautifully gowned ladies who moved in dignified procession to the church door, anything less like the Bishop's Chapel could hardly be imagined. At one side of the church, under the shade of the ancient trees that bordered the well-kept churchyard, there was quite a congregation of servants—footmen and chairmen, the former gorgeous in their livery, the latter glad of the chance of a Sunday morning gossip.

A solemn-faced verger showed the Aikenheads into their pew—capacious and comfortable with cushioned seats and hassocks for one's feet, and a formidable array of hymn books on a little shelf. Mary gravely sat up beside her father and had a good look round before the service began. Never had she found herself in such a fashionable assembly. The sunlight streaming through the windows glinted on the frocks of the ladies, while the constant rustle of silk and satin brought dreamily to her mind the buzzing of bees in the herbaceous border in Daddy John's garden. How different it all was! She noted the absence of statues and of the Stations; of the red lamp that burned before the Tabernacle; and of the flowers and shrines. Of the altar itself she could see little, because directly in front of her was a large lady wearing a wide-brimmed hat, which was surmounted by a long white plume. This waved about in a fascinating manner every time she moved and was a constant distraction to Mary during service. There was much hymn-singing, prayers in English, and a sermon preached by an earnest-looking young minister. Then followed more prayers and Mary joined her hands and closed her eyes and tried so hard to pray as Mammy had taught her to do when at Mass, but somehow the prayers wouldn't come. Her mind was distracted . . . wandering. . . . She opened her eyes and peeped sideways at her father to see what he was doing. The doctor was kneeling upright, very stiff and rigid.

" What is he thinking of?" she wondered. Then the white plume again claimed her attention and she watched it sway gently, this way and that till they stood up for the final hymn.

Outside the church, the doctor, bowing and smiling, allowed himself to be congratulated on his charming daughter, and Mary had her shoulder patted affectionately by elderly gentlemen in powdered wigs and had her rosy cheeks playfully pinched by the graceful white fingers of handsome ladies who declared her to be the image of her father. It was really a delightful ending to a pleasant morning, and Mary was almost sorry when the gay chattering congregation broke up and the sedan chairs and carriages began to move slowly away.

Hardly had Paddy whipped up the horses and the journey home begun when Mary voiced the question that was uppermost in her mind.

" Papa, did Jesus come down on that altar?" The doctor, whose thoughts happened to be on the Sunday dinner, was rather taken aback.

" Of course, my dear," he replied. " Jesus is God, and God is everywhere."

" Oh, yes, Papa, I know that, but when did He come specially down from Heaven? Mammy Rorke said that when the boy rang the little bell——"

" My dear child," interrupted her father, " Mrs. Rorke is a very good woman, an excellent woman, no doubt, but you mustn't take too seriously everything she says. People of her class have their heads filled with superstition——"

" Papa, what's superstition?" she demanded.

" Well—er—um—superstition is—ah—praying to images, lighting candles and er—ringing bells."

" But, Papa," she persisted, " is it wrong to ring a bell?"

The doctor realised that unless he took a firm stand he would find himself landed in a theological argument, which would perhaps involve his wife also, and the last thing he wanted to do was to stress any difference between Mrs. Aikenhead and himself.

" My dear Mary," he said decidedly, " religion is a subject that is very sacred and is never discussed in public. A person's beliefs are a matter between God Almighty and himself. He is answerable for his behaviour while on earth to God only and to nobody else."

If a question trembled on the little girl's lips it was not expressed. Her father's tone and general demeanour made it quite obvious to her that the discussion was closed—outwardly, that is, but inwardly her active young mind puzzled over it all, to come quietly in time to its own conclusions.

" Mammy," she asked one day, after she had been some time attending services at Shandon, " do you ever say any prayers for me now?"

" To be sure I do, Miss Mary," was the nurse's reply.

" Well, Mammy,' went on her darling, " don't say any more prayers for me on the small beads, say them only on the large ones."

" Indeed, Miss Mary, they're the very prayers I'll say for you and no other," and Mrs. Rorke continued to pray harder than ever before that " Holy Mary, Mother of God," would watch over and protect her own little girl.

About this time, Mrs. Stackpole, the children's grandmother, a dignified old lady and a devout Catholic, came to visit them. Since the question of religion was never mentioned in the house and since

Mary seemed to take her mother's non-appearance at church for granted, it is doubtful if she realised to the full what she was saying when on the occasion of Mrs. Stackpole's offering her a pretty Rosary and suggesting that it would be nice for her doll's house, Mary replied, after due consideration, and in a manner that left no doubt as to her meaning:

"No thank you, Grandmama. All my dolls go to church except the kitchen maid, and it's much too good for her."

Mother Aikenhead and her friend visiting the poor in Cork.

CHAPTER III

Daybreak

WITH FINGERS that shook slightly Mary fumbled for the heavy bolt; slowly and with infinite patience she worked it up and down, her heart almost missing a beat every time she made the slightest sound, lest even a squeak would betray her presence in the dark hallway. Ah!—there it was at last—now for the key, one turn, a slight click and the door swung open—another half-minute and she was on the street, her cloak drawn tightly around her, the hood pulled down well over her face, walking rapidly away from the house in the grey light of a January dawn. . . .

" In nomine Patris, et filii et spiritus sancti . . ."

The priest was just beginning Mass as she slipped into the little chapel and mingled with the other worshippers. Her head bent, her hands joined, she knelt in prayer without sound or movement. It was only when she stood erect at the Gospel and her hood fell back slightly from her face, that she was recognised in the dim candle-light. Yes, it was Dr. Aikenhead's eldest daughter, come to keep her tryst with One Who was wooing her gently, and to Whose pleading voice she could no longer turn a deaf ear.

* * * * * *

It was the year 1800 and many were the spiritual changes that had been wrought in Mary since the day when, as a little girl, she had refused the Rosary beads. Her grandmother, very wisely, had passed over the incident without comment and had merely invited the child to visit her at her own house, there to make the acquaintance of her mother's unmarried sisters and her brother Philip. The Stackpoles were a lively and friendly family, proud of the Clare and Limerick blood that ran in their veins. They were well-educated, musical, fond of society, and Mary had immediately taken a liking to their pleasing and unpretentious home. It had been quite a revelation to her to find that, since the Penal days, while the monopoly of civic and military distinction lay with the Protestants, Catholics had a host of compensations. Denied entrance to the clubs, they had society and companionship around their own hearths and at their own dinner tables. The better-class Catholics, and Mary was now beginning to find that there were such, in quite appreciable numbers, entertained one another hospitably. There were enjoyable evenings spent by Mary among the Stackpoles and their friends—the Hennesseys, the Roches and the McMahons—gatherings every bit as entertaining as those spent in the company of her father's guests. Indeed, they were more enjoyable as there was no standing on ceremony, since all present were on terms of equality.

The piety of the Stackpoles was worthy of their faith. They usually attended the chapel of the South Parish, which they had helped to rebuild, but Mrs. Stackpole herself was particularly fond of the old Bishop's Chapel. Mary, who greatly admired her grandmother, perhaps because she found in the older woman the strength of character that was missing in her mother, had gradually outgrown her former prejudices to the extent of asking if she might go with her to evening devotions. But so far was Mrs. Stackpole from influencing her grandchild in any way that her offer of a Rosary was never repeated; and Mary, who had come to love that form of prayer had made herself a decade by tying knots in her garter. This, however, could hardly be used in public, so the Hail Marys had, perforce, to be counted on her fingers when in chapel.

About this time there arrived from the Continent a widowed aunt named Mrs. Gorman, who was to have a profound influence on Mary's life. This lady, who from the time of her husband's death had lived almost the life of a religious, was a personal friend of the Bishop, Dr. Moylan, and was to take a great interest in her handsome young niece. Mary, who soon became very much attached to her aunt, had long talks on the subject of religion, borrowing books from her which she read with eagerness.

All this time a struggle had been going on in Mary's soul. On the one hand there was her father and his so obviously cultured and well-to-do friends, the cream of Cork society, and on the other hand there were the Stackpoles, in whose company, permeated as it was by the spirit of religion, she felt so much at home. She was living in a state

of divided loyalty and, young though she was, a child of eleven, sh
had realised that she must go one way or the other and that nobod
could make the decision but herself. The strain began to tell on he
and she had become unusually thoughtful for a girl of her age. He
gravity of manner and ever-growing seriousness had so far, however
attracted little notice, since the city itself was plunged in gloom, fo
that was the fateful year of 1798. Although there had been no out
break of rebellion in Cork, many of the citizens were mourning th
loss of relatives and friends; while the poor, who had none to defen
them, were living in constant dread of arrest and torture. Whippings
pitch-caps, half-hangings were the order of the day.

Politics, like religion, were never discussed in the Aikenhea
household, and for obvious reasons. The doctor dared not voice hi
sentiments openly, especially as some of the magistrates who wer
dealing so unjustly with the so-called rebels were his own friends an
acquaintances. Many were the fearful stories in circulation about th
dreadful punishments meted out to those whose only crime was tha
they had tried to fight for the freedom of their country, and Mar
sometimes had overheard gossip from the servants that struck terro
into her sensitive soul. In bed at night she would toss and turr
unable to sleep, picturing vividly the men who had been hanged an
whose heads had been fixed on spikes around the city gaol. The mor
she shut her eyes and tried to go to sleep, the more clearly she coul
see their faces.

One day a poor woman came to her father to beg ointment an
bandages for her son who had been flogged that morning with th
cat o' nine tails by order of the Sheriff, Dr. Harding. Mary met he
just outside the shop, and noticing her distress asked her the caus
of it, and the hot tears sprang to her own eyes on hearing the story

" Oh Miss Mary," the poor thing cried, " they tell me he's in a cru
state down there in the prison. Won't you pray they may let me i
to do something for him, my poor boy? The skin is stripped from hi
back. Oh Mother of God, 'tis awful. *She* knew what it was to hav
her Son ——". Here the quivering voice choked and the wretche
creature shuffled away, while Mary stood looking after her, miser
and resentment mingling in her heart.

" If only I could go and comfort him," she thought. " The poo
are always the ones to suffer and no one seems to mind what happen
to them. It's shameful! It's unfair!"

And turning, she had run into the house, up the stairs past an astonished housemaid, who had never before seen her young mistress in such agitation, into her bedroom, where she slammed the door and flinging herself on her knees, took up her little garter and began to pray.

In the same year Dr. Aikenhead, though by no means an elderly man, had decided to retire from professional work. Hardworking all his life, he had amassed sufficient money to enable him to sell his practice and enjoy a life of greater ease. Whatever happened, he would be able to leave his family well provided for. There would be comfortable marriage settlements for his daughters, while his son, whose health was giving cause for anxiety, could have every care and treatment that the medical skill of that time provided.

In due course the establishment of Aikenhead and Dupont had changed hands, and then had followed the excitement of moving to a new house. The semi-picnic existence one lives when packing is in progress appealed to the children. What a thrill it was to sit on stools or even boxes to a makeshift meal and then to find there weren't enough plates or spoons to go round! What fun to have no carpets on the floors, no pictures on the walls; to have the hall piled high with tables, chairs, pots and pans; to have strange men staggering downstairs under heavy loads. Why, there couldn't be more fuss if one were going to Dublin—a journey which, to the younger children at any rate, would have meant like going to Timbuctoo.

Finally their old home was bare and the children and Mrs. Rorke, who had stayed to see the last man safely off the premises, prepared to depart for their new home in Rutland Street, whither Dr. and Mrs. Aikenhead had already gone with the rest of the domestic staff to begin the task of unpacking and settling in.

" Come along children," Mammy cried, " 'tis time we were going."

They trooped after her into the hall, their footsteps resounding eerily through the empty house. Mary lingered a moment outside her father's study. Never again would she steal in on tiptoe and pounce suddenly upon him and cry, in what she always hoped was a disguised voice, " Guess who it is." Never again would he play up to her and enjoy her suppressed giggles as he guessed almost every notable person in the city before he asked at last, " Is it my own little girlie?" Never again would she sit on his knee in this dear, familiar, untidy room, put her arms round his neck and coax a bottle of medicine for a poor sick friend. Never again. . . . But here Mrs. Rorke, calling from the door, had put an end to her thoughts, and she had moved to join the others, who could talk of nothing but of the wonderful time they would have in their new house.

When they moved to Rutland Street, Mary, then twelve years of age, asked her aunt to take her to Mass. Her aunt complied with her request, and one morning when Mass was followed by Benediction of the Most Blessed Sacrament, Mary, who was deeply impressed, questioned Mrs. Gorman closely in order that she might learn more about the Mass and Benediction. From this there grew up in her a longing to attend Mass every morning. How to do this without causing any trouble was a problem. She discovered without much difficulty that in a chapel (the Catholics were never allowed to use the word "church") not far from the house, there was Mass at half-past seven each morning and that, if she hurried home very quickly, she could be just in time for breakfast. It was worth trying any way, so enlisting the aid of a friendly housemaid, whose duties occasioned her presence in the vicinity of the hall door at that early hour, she had set off on that January morning. It was her first response to the Heavenly Lover's call.

* * * * * *

The priest had barely left the altar when she rose to her feet and swiftly left the chapel, hoping against hope that she had not been missed at home. The return journey was beset with perils; she dared not walk too rapidly for fear of attracting attention, yet, if she were late. . . . Once she thought with dismay that all was lost! A gentleman friend of her father's was approaching her, on the same side of the street, too, and the pavement was so narrow! Surely, he would recognise her as he passed . . . but no! Though he almost brushed against her he did not appear to notice her.

"A miracle—a miracle," she thought, but actually the miracle had a very simple explanation, for she had borrowed Mammy Rorke's cloak, and none of her father's friends would ever have looked twice at the shabby figure that slipped by in it.

She was breathless when at last she reached the door. With her knuckles she gave a soft tap-tap-tap, the pre-arranged signal, pray-

Their Temporal Neec

ing fervently that Kitty would hear. Quietly the door opened. With a sigh of relief she slipped inside.

"Quick, Miss Mary, I'll take your cloak," said the girl. "You're only just in time."

With a grateful smile, Mary tripped into the dining-room. "Good morning, Papa and Mama," she gaily cried. Now that she had done it once it would never be so hard again.

Dr. Aikenhead did not live long to enjoy his life of retirement. Towards the end of the year 1801 he became seriously ill, and by Christmas there was no hope of his recovery. The minister came and prayed with him, offering him such consolation as his Church could provide. The dying man received it gratefully, but his mind was not at ease. He was restless and unhappy. Meanwhile, his wife, with Mary, Mrs. Rorke and a whole host of Catholic friends, rich and poor, were praying unceasingly for him. Of his own accord he asked to see a priest. After some serious conversations, his doubts vanished and he begged to be received into the Catholic Church. He died on December 28th while his family, the Bishop and faithful Mammy Rorke knelt around his bed. Death brought joy as well as sorrow to those who loved him.

Light was beginning to stream into Mary's soul, for her father's conversion and very happy death had impressed her deeply. Success in life, wealth, social position, honour, respect had all been her father's to enjoy throughout life, and yet when it came to the end they had mattered nothing to him. In the one thing necessary, and in that alone, he had only found peace and comfort. Hers it was now to choose the better part; yet she wavered, and it was not until she heard a sermon preached by Dr. Florence MacCarthy on the parable of Dives and Lazarus that she made the final decision.

Yes, she, too, knew many people "clad in purple and fine linen who feasted sumptuously." There were hundreds of them this day in the City of Cork, unmindful of the beggars who lay in hunger and misery, cold and nakedness, if not at their very gates, at least in the lanes, the alleys, the hovels within a stone's throw of their comfortable homes. These poor, the lowly, the despised, were the people who were dear to the Heart of Jesus. With these she would cast in her lot. Henceforth, whatever she possessed in the way of "purple and fine linen" she would share with them; never again would she feast sumptuously without setting aside a portion for some poor Lazarus. Had not Christ said: "As long as you did it to one of these my least brethren you did it to me"?

Once her mind was made up she confided to her aunt: "I'll never be happy until I am a Catholic;" to which the good lady replied without more ado: "Why not become one now?"

Straightaway her instructions began, and on June 6th, 1802, she was received into the Church. On the 29th she made her First Holy Communion. Then on July 2nd she became, through Confirmation, a strong and perfect Christian, who would be faithful to Christ unto death. Her darkness of soul was at an end.

CHAPTER IV

Lavender and Lace

THE GIRL from West Cork sighed rapturously. " Isn't it beautiful? I never saw the beat of it," and she leaned out farther over the balcony.

" Be careful," whispered her companion. " There'll be a fine hub-bub if you fall down, and mind they don't see you; we shouldn't really be here at all."

Nonie obediently drew back a little and, crouched in the sheltering darkness of the gallery, the two girls feasted their eyes on the gay scene below.

" But, of course," she went on, " in London they have balls nearly every night of the week, and the dresses are far more stylish than in Cork. When I was there last year . . ."

Here her voice trailed away into silence as she realised that Nonie wasn't listening to her; that young damsel, in spirit at any rate, had joined the group of dancers in the hall below. No longer was she plain little Nonie Murphy from the back o' beyond, come up to the city to be in service, with a black dress, white apron and mob cap; instead she was one of the ladies, one of the prettiest, too, in her rustling silk ball-dress and tiny golden shoes, dancing with the handsomest man in the room. Her gaze wandered over the brightly-clad figures of the men. There was a goodly sprinkling of military and naval officers resplendent in their uniforms of scarlet and blue, trimmed with gold braid; but no, her gallant partner would be neither a soldier nor a sailor. At last her eyes rested on a young gentleman wearing a plum-coloured satin coat and black velvet knee breeches, with a cravat, lace ruffles and silk stockings of purest white. From the top of his powdered head to the twinkling buckles on his shoes he was a typical Prince Charming. The musicians were playing a minuet now, and it was a delight to watch his graceful figure. Nonie, tapping with her foot in time to the music, became conscious, rather ruefully, of her own clumsy boots and woollen stockings. Critically she examined his partner, a rosy-faced, well-built young lady in a full-skirted white lace dress with a lavender sash, and shoes. She, too, was a graceful dancer, and they seemed to be thoroughly enjoying themselves.

" Who's he?" demanded Nonie suddenly.

" Sh-sh-sh, go easy, which one?" whispered Annie cautiously.

" Him over by the window."

" Oh, that one, is it, dancing with Miss Aikenhead? He's Sir Richard Graham."

" I think he looks lovely," murmured Nonie dreamily. " Who'd you say she is?"

" Miss Aikenhead, a nice young lady she is, too. No airs or graces about her."

There was silence in the gallery. Nonie closed her eyes. . . . Down in the ballroom softly radiant with honey-coloured candle-light Miss Nonie Murphy danced with Sir Richard Graham, who cast many admiring glances at her, and whispered little compliments which she blushingly acknowledged. He was just about to kiss her hand when—

" Wake up, little goose," came Annie's hoarse whisper. " We daren't stay any longer or we'll be missed." And poor Nonie, rudely awakened from her dream stumbled in the dark after her companion, her thoughts still dwelling on foamy lace ruffles and buckled shoes.

With a low bow from the gentlemen and a deep curtsey from the ladies, the minuet came to an end, and after a polite round of applause, the girl with the lavender sash, joined by Cecilia, Eileen and her other special friends, found themselves seats in a vacant corner. Similar groups of white-clad girls were dotted here and there around the room while the gentlemen, taking advantage of the brief interval, repaired to the garden for a breath of fresh air and a chat and, one of them at least, to rehearse a speech he intended making to a very pretty young lady, to be followed, of course, by a most important question. . . . What if she should refuse? Already he was going hot and cold at the mere prospect of such a calamity. Some moments later he noticed that the other gentlemen were moving towards the ballroom. Taking his courage in both hands he strode after them, making his way through the laughing throng to where the very pretty young lady was waiting for him with a fluttering heart.

"Here he comes. Oh, dear, what shall I do?" she whispered to her companion.

"Say 'yes,' of course," answered that young person promptly. Then, as her own partner came for her: "I'll be praying for you," and with a twirl of her lavender sash, she was gone, while Eileen blushingly listened to a young man stammeringly suggest that as the night was very warm a walk in the garden would be pleasant.

The band struck up and a vigorous country dance began, so their departure was unnoticed by the lively couples hopping and skipping on the floor, but it was not so with the elderly folk, who, seated around the wall in armchairs and roomy couches, kept a wary eye on the young people to see that the conventions were well observed. Not indeed that they were chaperons in the strict sense of the word, for society in Cork was of a pleasantly free and easy nature. Everybody knew everybody else, and all about them, too! Religious prejudices also had become less owing to the fact that so many Protestants and Presbyterians were in sympathy with the United Ireland movement, and it was not surprising that the sons and daughters of well-off Catholic parents should be present at balls and parties given by families who, ten or fifteen years earlier, would have cut them dead on the street.

Behind their fans and under cover of the lids of snuff-boxes a running commentary of all that took place was kept up by the fond papas and mamas, aunts and uncles as they relived their own romances in the love affairs of the younger generation. Matches were made and remade; the merits and demerits of the various young people were argued about, sometimes with considerable heat, since opinions greatly differed as to what were the requirements necessary to make a good wife or husband.

"Mark my words," said one stout gentleman, "poor Aikenhead's girl will do well for herself. A fine capable young woman with a head on her shoulders, not like some of the giddy creatures here to-night."

"No," agreed his friend, taking a pinch of snuff, "she's a kind heart, too; wouldn't object to having her for a daughter-in-law myself. John is none too steady y' know. A girl of her character would make him pull himself together. She wouldn't nag at him either!"

" Pray, sir, when were you nagged at?" demanded his wife, " and if John is not steady, who's to blame for it?"

Her husband meekly subsided, amid covert smiles from the other ladies who knew all about his little weakness, and the subject was tactfully changed by bringing some other young lady under discussion, while the girl with the lavender sash danced gaily on, not caring what anyone thought or said of her, thinking only of Eileen and praying for her as she had promised.

Down in the kitchen it was a case of " all hands on deck." Parlour maids and even ladies' maids were pressed into service on a night like this, and so it happened that Nonie up to the elbows in greasy water, was still weaving romances around Sir Richard to the accompaniment of rattling plates, knives and forks as the busy girls hurried through their work in order to get up to the gallery, where they were always permitted to go once they had finished downstairs.

" You're just longing to get back, aren't you?" remarked Annie, coming with a cloth to help in the drying. " When I was like you I thought I couldn't see enough of them, but now I'm quite used to it all."

" Were you ever like me?" asked Nonie in amazement. " I thought you were always a lady's maid."

" Indeed, no," replied Annie. " When I came here ten years ago I hadn't a boot to my foot, and the mistress had to dress me."

" You don't say!" cried Nonie, thinking hopefully that in time to come there might even be a chance for her. She, too, might travel abroad with her young lady and, perhaps, even learn to speak French like Annie, who could say " Oui, Madame " and " Non, M'sieu " and " Pardonnez," and a great deal more besides.

" If you want to get on," came Annie's voice firmly, " you'll have to stop being dreamy; do be quick, or we'll never get upstairs."

Nonie's red little hands began to move rapidly in and out of the water, 'twould never do if she didn't see Sir Richard and—and——

" Is he goin' to marry Miss Aikenhead?" she demanded.

" Who—Sir Richard Graham? Well," replied Annie, weighing her words, " he might be goin' to marry her, but she's not goin' to marry him."

"Oh, dear! Are you sure?" The West Cork accent was tinged with anxiety.

"Sure and certain I am," declared Annie, "and you may put that idea out of your head. 'Twas my own gran told me."

"Your gran?"

"Yes, she's been lyin' these two years with a bad leg, an 'ulster' she calls it, and Miss Aikenhead goes to see her every mornin' nearly. She's terrible kind entirely, and one day there, not so long ago, my gran said to her: ''Twill be the lucky man'll get you, Miss Mary.'"

"'Now Granny Doyle,' said she, 'you mustn't talk like that. 'Tis no man'll get me,' and she smiled kind of queer."

"An' what did she mean? Who's goin' to get her?"

"God," answered Annie impressively. "She's goin' to be a nun."

"But what about Sir Richard? Doesn't he love her?" cried Nonie in dismay.

"I s'pose so, but he'll get over it; his kind always does. Come along now, dry your hands and hurry up!"

The last minuet was in progress as they reached the gallery, Nonie's tender heart sore at the thought of the lover's disappointment. She pictured him lonely and disconsolate outside the convent wall. What a sad thing love was, to be sure, and she looked with increased interest at the girl with the lavender sash, so happy, so full of life and yet . . . .

A few minutes more and the ball was over. Then came the gay farewells. The elderly ladies were conducted to their sedan chairs while the younger folk, putting on heavy shoes and cloaks, were escorted home in groups under the guardianship of a father or elder brother led by a servant carrying a lantern, for unless there was a moon the streets were inky black.

Mary, who loved the walk home under the starlight, so cool and pleasant after the heat of the ballroom, was standing at the door waiting for the rest of their party when she felt a slight touch on her arm.

"It's all right," came Eileen's soft voice. "I said 'yes,' and Mary, I'm so happy. I want you to know first. He asked Papa yesterday and he says we may be married next year. Isn't it wonderful!"

"I'm so glad," whispered Mary, squeezing her hand, "so very glad."

" And," added Eileen hesitantly, " I hope that when you're asked you'll be as—as happy."

" Even happier," said Mary, smiling to herself in the darkness. " God bless you, my dear."

They made a merry group on the way home; their voices ringing out on the still night air awakened some of the more sober-minded citizens, and once a bedroom window was slammed in protest at the youthful disturbers of the peace. Just as they were passing a narrow lane in the vicinity of Rutland Street, Mary, who was walking with her friend Cecilia Lynch, stopped suddenly, as though listening to something.

" What is the matter?" asked her friend.

" I thought I heard a call," replied Mary. " There it is again. Listen!" And the two girls dropped back a little from the others, who passed on unheeding.

Cecilia heard it clearly now, the feeble wail of a child. " Poor little thing," she murmured compassionately, " it's hungry. We must come here in the morning," for they spent several hours every day visiting the poor, and if there was hardly a lane or alley way unknown to them, neither were they unknown to the most forsaken old woman or most wretched of beggars, nor to the unkempt and ragged starvelings who would come peeping into their baskets—human sparrows looking for crumbs.

They did what they could to relieve their wants but it was all so little, so pitifully inadequate, in the face of the utter poverty met on every side. Mary had lived amongst the poor in her early youth on Eason's Hill—the respectable hardworking poor, but now she was coming across another type of poverty, more properly called destitution, and she was daily realising, ever more clearly, that her efforts and those of her friends were almost useless. If anything really worth while was to be done to better their condition it would have to be through some organised channel, such as a Society or Congregation set up for that purpose.

Already she was feeling the urge to devote her life to their service, not as a mere Lady Bountiful but as a religious sister; not from afar off behind convent walls but in their midst—on the streets and in their homes. How it was to be managed she did not know; the whole point of consecrating oneself to God meant separation from the world, not mixing with it. The difficulty was to reconcile the two ideas, to be a nun in the world but not of it.

Mary went to sleep that night not with the haunting air of a minuet but with the cry of a hungry child ringing in her ears. But it was not only a cry: it was a call—a call that would have to be answered somehow, sometime.

In Lighter Vein.

CHAPTER V

A Bird of Passage

THE MAIL coach drew up with a jerk that shook all the occupants out of their uneasy doze; all of them, that is, except one stout old gentleman in the corner whose prodigious snores droned on. A great deal of yawning and stretching ensued as the cramped and weary passengers tried to ease their positions. The rustling and shifting of feet mingled with the sounds outside—the driver stamping about the yard, the steaming horses greedily sucking up water. All too short was the respite till the driver, with a final stamp and much rubbing of hands, mounted again and began the last stage of the long journey from Cork which would end at the Post Office, College Green, Dublin.

Mary Aikenhead, now wide awake, sat bolt upright. She could hardly do otherwise, as she was tightly wedged between two ladies, one of whom was so ample of build as to be almost cushionlike, while the other was so angular that she seemed to be all elbows and knees, as Mary found to her cost with the constant rolling of the top-heavy coach.

With every turn of the wheels her spirits soared higher, for was she not drawing nearer and nearer to her goal? Time passes very slowly when a young lady is in her 'teens and early twenties, especially when she sees her friends, one by one, settled and happy in their various vocations while she herself, as a bird of passage, flits here and there with a still undecided future. So it had been with Mary, but now she hoped the uncertainty was at an end.

Tucked into the bosom of her dress was the letter from her dearest Anna Maria inviting her to Dublin. That in itself was nothing new, for Mary had had several trips already to the Capital and was quite a seasoned traveller. But the letter also told her that in the near future no less a person than the Coadjutor Archbishop himself was to found a Community of Sisters of Charity, nuns who would live amongst the poor and spend themselves and be spent in their service. Dr. Murray was no stranger to Mary. Many times on her previous visits to Dublin they had met to discuss this very point. Mary had confided to Anna Maria that as soon as he could gather together a little band of women interested in the same cause under the guidance of an efficient superior, she would have no hesitation in joining them.

The long delay had only strengthened her vocation and had helped to increase and foster her tender charity towards the poor. Amid the busy duties of running a house, bringing up her younger sisters—her mother was dead some years—and the paying of social calls incidental to her state, she had never omitted her daily excursions through the miry lanes and up and down the rickety stairs.

Once, at least, her acts of kindness took a highly novel form. On her way home in the evening she noticed a poor apple woman crying behind her stall of unsold fruit while the vendors around her were doing a roaring trade. When she asked the cause, Mary was told that these particular apples were a ha'penny dearer than those on the other stalls. The rent was due that night so the poor creature's plight could hardly have been worse. In an instant Miss Aikenhead herself set to work and the pile of fruit steadily decreased. But, of course, the story did not end there; explanations had to be given to mothers and curious sisters as to why their menfolk had suddenly decided to come home with pockets full of apples! Naturally some applauded her kind action while others raised their white bejewelled hands and with horrified eyes announced to all and sundry that they didn't know what the younger generation was coming to! As for that Miss Aikenhead, well, she was surely going to the dogs with her gadabout ways!

While Mary was jogging along in the mail coach, dreaming rosy dreams and building convents in the air, her " dearest Anna Maria," Mrs. John O'Brien, living in what was then the fashionable district of Mountjoy Square, eagerly awaited the arrival of her young visitor. They had taken a strong liking to each other from the first meeting in Cork several years ago. Mrs. O'Brien belonged to the only class of Catholics that had any worldly prosperity, that of the merchants and traders. Her husband, a rich and generous man, encouraged his wife in her works of charity by placing large sums of money at her disposal. Their house was the centre of Catholic Society, in which her gaiety and charm made her a brilliant figure. Yet for all that her chief interest in life lay in helping the poor and advancing the cause of the oppressed and persecuted Church.

The penal laws had done their work well, and in spite of the fact that O'Connell had already begun his great work for emancipation, centuries of ill-treatment and injustice had reduced the majority of her co-religionists to a state of servility. Deprived of their language, their education, their property, they were a race of half-starved illiterates from whom everything had been filched except their Faith. To this they clung tenaciously despite the threats of "dungeon, fire and sword." Their chapels were barns hidden away at the back of taverns or hucksters' shops, approached by narrow laneways. Their schools were few. Hundreds upon hundreds of poor children, little better than vagabonds, ran about the streets. However, if the Catholics were ignorant of the finer points of doctrine, the light of Faith burned clearly in their souls. They showed wonderful trust in God, absolute conformity to His will, patient endurance in suffering. A glorious harvest was waiting to be reaped, but where were the labourers?

Mrs. O'Brien—known by her friends as a "Sister of Charity living in the world"—did all she could by visiting the poor herself and interesting others on their behalf; by founding a House of Refuge in Ashe Street to save girls from evil influences; by trying to encourage the better-class Catholics to take the place, originally theirs by right, in the social life of the country. With this last end in view she dressed beautifully, entertained royally and drove to Mass in state.

For the tenth time that afternoon she opened the door of the bedroom prepared for Mary and peeped in to see that everything was in order. 'Twouldn't be long now. Her carriage had already set off to meet the mail, and she noted with satisfaction the brightly blazing fire, the comfortable bed with the clothes turned back and a warming pan between the sheets, the jug of hot water and fresh clean towels. No, there was nothing forgotten; then, as her quick ear caught the sound of wheels, she hastened down the stairs to have the joy of opening the door herself to the tired and weary traveller.

"May I come in, my dear?" It was some hours later and Mary, refreshed in body and contented in soul, was lying awake idly watching the firelight dance on the walls and waiting for Mrs. O'Brien to come for her promised chat. Her kind hostess had insisted on her retiring immediately but had agreed to look in after supper.

"Oh yes, do," she answered eagerly. "Is it very late? I feel as if I've been asleep for hours."

"And so you have," smiled Anna Maria. "This is the third time I've come to the door. It's gone ten o'clock now so I musn't stay long," seating herself on a low stool close to the fire.

"Now tell me all," Mary begged, and Mrs. O'Brien had to give an account of everything that had transpired since they last met and of the Archbishop's plans for the future. It was almost eleven before she finished, but even then Mary was not satisfied. Sitting up in bed, a white shawl round her shoulders, her curly hair hanging loosely about her face, she looked more like a girl of sixteen than a young woman of twenty-four. Question followed question. Just the faintest shadow passed over Mrs. O'Brien's face when Mary remarked: "It's strange Dr. Murray hasn't said anything about the Rev. Mother. I wonder who can she be?" Mrs. O'Brien tried to steady her voice as she answered casually:

"That's a secret yet, I believe," then, coming over to the bed, she took the shawl from Mary's shoulders, made her lie down and started to tuck her up.

"You'll know to-morrow when His Grace calls. Is there anyone you would suggest?"

"Yes," came the immediate reply, "you, my dearest Anna Maria."

"Foolish child, and what about my poor John?" kissing her and tracing the Sign of the Cross on her forehead. "God bless you and make you do great things for Him."

To which Mary gave a sleepy "Amen."

Dr. Murray, Archbishop of Hieropolis and Coadjutor to the See of Dublin, presented himself at Mrs. O'Brien's house the following afternoon and asked for an interview with Miss Aikenhead.

Dignified and stately in bearing, gentle and courteous in manner, with luminous dark eyes that could see into the depths of one's soul, he bore a reputation amongst his brother clergy for more than ordinary holiness, while to the poverty stricken children of his flock he showed unwearying tenderness and devotion.

Outside the drawing room door Mary paused a moment, her heart overflowing with gratitude to God that at last He was about to make His will known to her, and begging that she, too, might be considered worthy to be numbered amongst the members of the future congregation of the Sisters of Charity. She tapped lightly, then entered.

It was not a long interview as interviews go, but when it was over and His Grace had gone, a very different Mary went slowly to her bedroom and knelt, crucifix in hand, in silent prayer. How could she face those tasks of heavy responsibility which the Archbishop would insist on entrusting to her?

It was indeed a very solemn young lady who boarded the mail coach for Cork some ten days or so later. Even the gruff joviality of the driver and the backchat of the guard failed to raise the flicker of a smile in the serious dark grey eyes. As the coach jolted and rattled its way over the stony road she leaned her head against the back of the seat and closed her eyes. Not that she was going to sleep but that she was determined to avoid the possibility of being drawn into conversation by her fellow travellers. In her mind she went back over the words spoken at that momentous interview. She experienced again the sensation she felt then—the ground slipping away from under her feet and herself sinking, sinking down as the full meaning of what Dr. Murray was saying dawned upon her. There was *no* convent, *no* group of pious ladies, *no* superior, other than herself! Her tears and her protests that such a position was quite beyond her powers had left the Archbishop unmoved. She and no one else was to be the foundress and first superior. In vain she had pleaded and put forward every argument against her suitability. He had listened patiently to all she had to say and had only replied that he would give her a few days to think about it, and if after that she could not bring herself to accept what he firmly believed to be the will of God for her, the idea of the prospective foundation would have to be dropped.

Mary had prayed as she had never done before. She would have fasted also with extreme rigour had it not been for the watchful eye of Mrs. O'Brien. Together they made a pilgrimage to the Poor Clare Convent, Harold's Cross, where Cecilia Lynch was a nun, to beg prayers that a " terrible calamity " might be averted. The inmates of the House of Refuge got a similar request. Their prayers, however, were not answered in her way but in God's, for, after opening her soul to Dr. Murray in a general confession, it had been borne in upon her that *this* really was His will for her. He Himself was asking her to bear this cross for Him, so she could not refuse.

In years to come she would write these words: " Sisters of Charity are not to gain Heaven without suffering, with as well for, the poor." Her sorrow had now begun. She accepted generously, and peace, if not joy, flooded her soul. Joy would come later but at the moment, as the coach moved along the winding country roads, she felt dismally that life would never be the same again. How could she ever be gay and lighthearted with such a burden weighing her down? It was all such a sad business and her thoughts were tinged with a gentle melancholy.

It had been settled by Doctor Murray that she should go back to Cork and teach her sisters how to take charge of the house. Meanwhile he would arrange to have a companion and herself accepted in a convent, probably in England, where they would be trained in the principles and practice of religious life, before returning to Dublin as the first Sisters of Charity.

There was consolation in the thought that for the moment, at any rate, there could be no question of making her a superior. There would be a respite of two years, or even more, and who could tell what might happen before then? God was good and she could trust Him, whatever happened, to provide. He who clothes the lilies of the field and feeds the ravens and takes care of the sparrows, could He not make an " efficient superior " out of the most unpromising material? Of course He could if only she would trust Him and believe in His love for her.

As the coach rounded a bend and she felt the comforting warmth of the setting sun full on her face she decided that life might not be so very hopeless after all, and that the very best way to trust God was to try and be happy about whatever He sent her. She would do what she could; He would not fail to do the rest. She relaxed her tensed attitude, opened her eyes and smiled, a trifle wanly, at the countrywoman opposite, who, she discovered, was looking at her in some concern.

" I thought you was poorly, Miss," she said apologetically, embarrassed at having been caught out staring at a lady.

" I was not very well," admitted Mary, " but," and her smile grew brighter, " I'm better now, very much better."

* * * * * *

" Good-bye, dearest sisters, you will be ever in my heart and prayers.

" Good-bye, my native city, and you, people of Cork, whose kindness I can never repay.

" Good-bye, Ireland, loveliest of lands."

The seagulls soared and swooped around the ship as she ploughed her way through the water. Mary stood watching the coast fade slowly away, till it was swallowed up in the mist and there was nothing to be seen but the green heaving sea stretching out, it seemed, to the very rim of the world. Their frail vessel was but a tiny speck on its vast bosom. Forcing back the tears that had sprung to her eyes, she thought of home and the dear familiar faces left behind. On Trinity Sunday, May 24th, 1812, she bade farewell to Cork and with it to the past with all its happiness. She offered herself to God forever to do whatever He might demand.

She and her companion, Alicia Walsh, who had been accepted by Dr. Murray for the proposed congregation, were on their way to York, where the Archbishop had arranged for them to enter the novitiate of the Institute of the Blessed Virgin Mary at Micklegate Bar. This had seemed to him the most suitable convent for training future Sisters of Charity, since the nuns were not strictly enclosed, but went out to visit the sick poor, an unusual thing in those days. He himself was travelling with them in order to hand them over personally to the Rev. Mother, who had already written kindly words of welcome to the Irish postulants.

So Mary had turned away from the " fair hills of Holy Ireland." Her hand was " to the plough " and there would be no looking back. With firm steps she walked along the deck to where Alicia stood, and together they tried to combat the waves of loneliness breaking over their souls.

CHAPTER VI

Merrie England

IN A room on the top storey of a house just outside the Micklegate Bar, York, a group of young ladies sat sewing industriously, while one of their number read aloud from a book that must have been of special interest, for every face, though still, was set and tense. It was the novices' room at St. Mary's Convent, and the young ladies were aspirants to the religious life. Some indeed, already received, wore the white veils of the novices; others, more recent arrivals, had the black muslin caps and veils of the postulants. Among these were Mary Aikenhead and Alicia Walsh who had entered some days previously, on June 6th, 1812. The book that was holding their attention was the French translation of a spiritual classic by Father Alphonsus Rodriguez, of the Society of Jesus. On this great work the souls of novices the wide world over have been nourished since the 16th century. In English it would have borne a high-sounding title, " The Practice of Christian and Religious Perfection," but among the novices the only name by which it was ever likely to be known was " Rod," an affectionate diminutive of the revered author's name.

In and out flashed the needles, on and on went the reader's voice, buffeting with hard North of England accent the exquisite French. Not that anybody minded; standards of French pronunciation in noviceships are not normally too exacting! At last a senior novice said, " Deo Gratias " in a low voice, the signal that the period allotted to Spiritual Reading was at an end. All rose; each novice and postulant carefully folded her work; scissors, cotton, stray pins and needles were collected and tidily put away by the Sister in charge. By the time a distant bell was heard all were in readiness to walk to the chapel with head bent decorously forward, with noiseless step, with eyes fixed modestly on the ground.

Mary Aikenhead found it difficult at first to keep her gaze from wandering and her tongue from wagging, there was so much to be seen and asked about. She envied Alicia, who seemed already quite a model of perfection—had she not once or twice taken it on herself to reprove Mary for her curiosity? And, oh, those novices! So well-versed did they appear in spiritual matters that both the newcomers regarded them as saints; their well-regulated movements, their controlled voices, their religious demeanour—there, surely, was the very hall-mark of sanctity! How amazed and unbelieving Mary would have been had she been told then that one day her picture would be hanging on the wall of that same novices' room, and that generations of young religious would be told of the Mother Foundress of an Irish congregation " who came to make her noviceship with us."

From the first moment that Dr. Murray presented his Irish postulants to the Rev. Mother they felt quite at home. It could hardly have been otherwise, because of the genuine warmth of the welcome they had received. His choice of the Bar Convent as a training ground for those destined to carry the message of God's love and mercy into " darkest Ireland " was indeed a happy one, as the convent had borne an enviable name for sanctity for well more than a hundred years. It was situated in a city which had been the rallying-point for the North of England Catholics and whose streets, more than once, ran red with martyrs' blood.

The house, built in 1685, continued as a convent in spite of the waves of persecution. At one period it was the only convent school in the whole of England. For a hundred and twenty years the nuns wore secular dress and did not dare to call themselves by religious names. It was only at the outbreak of the French Revolution, when some communities sought shelter in England and were hospitably received, that the York nuns ventured to emerge from their catacomb and appear overground. Not five minutes' walk from the convent stood St. Michael's Gate or the Micklegate Bar, where the heads of numerous martyrs had once been stuck on poles. A little farther away, on the Ouse Bridge, was the Tolbooth, where the first woman martyr of England, Margaret Clitherow, had suffered for the Faith in 1586. She had been placed lying on the ground, a sharp stone under her back, a heavy oak door on top, and then large stones had been hurled upon the door until she was crushed to death. One of her hands was preserved as a relic in the chapel. About half a mile outside the city was the York Tyburn, where in 1679 an old priest, Fr. Nicholas Postgate, was hanged, drawn and quartered, and where scores of priests and laymen, before his day and after it, won the martyr's crown, while many others died as the result of the cruel treatment inflicted on them in the evil-smelling dungeons of York Castle.

Small wonder then, that this place, rich in holy and heroic traditions, appealed to Mary's ardent nature. Perhaps she now realised, as never before, that the monopoly of suffering for the Faith did not lie with the people of her own country; that England, too, had her Penal Days and that those who kept the pearl of faith had paid a great price for it, in the prison cell, on the rack, the block or the gallows.

Far sooner than she expected, Mary Aikenhead settled down to noviceship life and rapidly acquired that religious decorum which had looked so difficult at the start. Never one to do things by halves, she put the whole force of mind, heart and will into the study and practice of the religious life. Every moment of her time that was not devoted to prayer or to noviceship tasks was spent in preparing herself for the great work that lay ahead. Because of this ultimate purpose she received special permission, not commonly accorded to postulants, to copy spiritual papers, translate books on the religious life, and make a detailed study of the Rule followed by the institute. Later on Dr. Murray sent from Paris the Rule of the Sisters of Charity founded by St. Vincent de Paul, but after a novena for guidance had been made by the whole convent, the latter Rule was rejected in favour of the former, although no final decision was taken for some time to come.

Haunted by the thought of the authority soon to be thrust upon her, Mary would have become over-anxious in her efforts to attain perfection were it not for the kindly sympathy of her Novice Mistress, Mother Austin Chalmers. A wise and holy woman, she fully appreciated the mental strain which her Irish " daughter " was bearing, and lightened it with every means in her power. Mary Aikenhead had yet a long way to go before acquiring the unruffled serenity and calm acceptance of God's will, which afterwards was one of her outstanding characteristics.

In due course the term as postulants ended, and Mary and Alicia were received as novices. Although they were now called, respectively,

Sister Mary Augustine and Sister Mary Catherine, they did not put on the religious habit of the institute; rather did they continue to wear the postulant's dress, black cap and veil. The months slipped quietly and uneventfully by, the only contact with the outside world being letters from home and from Dr. Murray. The former were sometimes an added source of anxiety, for the Aikenhead girls were not proving as capable in the house or in matters financial as their eldest sister had been. Those from the Archbishop were full of encouragement and counsel, but neither did they fail to carry reproof when such was considered to be necessary. Once Mary wrote to him about her fears of being made Superior; for this, she said she would be utterly unfit. His letter in reply was long and very spiritual; it exhorted her to generosity and confidence in God, to joy in His service, to growth in the spirit of fervour, while towards the end there came the following lines: "Allow me to remark that there may be sometimes as much humility in accepting an office as in rejecting it. Where there is true humility there is no obstinate self-will. . . ." "Obstinate self-will!" she had never looked at it like that before. Off she went to the chapel, made her Act of Contrition and prayed for the virtue of humility! She had learnt her lesson; never more would a reprimand of this kind be necessary.

The chief work of the Institute of the Blessed Virgin Mary being that of education, a certain part of the novices' training was given to teaching, so after some time Sister Mary Augustine and Sister Mary Catherine found themselves appointed to take classes in Christian doctrine, reading, spelling and arithmetic.

"Black Monday" came, and Sister Mary Augustine, trembling at the ordeal that lay before her, walked into the classroom some ten or fifteen minutes before the bell for school, ostensibly to look over some lesson books, in reality to gather her wits together. Early as she was, she was not long without company. Presently she became aware of a rustling noise, followed by whispering and stifled giggles. She gave a rapid glance round the room; it was empty. But then her eye fell on the door which was slightly ajar, though she had shut it carefully some moments before.

"She's there," came a muffled voice. "Can you see her, Belle?"

"No, I can't. Your head is in the way—oh! mind my foot! Yes, I can see her now—do stop pushing!"

There was a further scuffle and suppressed laughter. Sister

Augustine went swiftly to the door, threw it open and two little girls almost tumbled into the room. One was a fair-headed, blue-eyed, sturdy child of ten; the other, of a more fragile build, was very dark, olive-complexioned with black dancing eyes. They looked at her curiously. Neither spoke.

"Good morning, children," said the novice at last, thinking it was time for her to say something.

"There, I told you so," said the dark one triumphantly. "I knew she'd speak English." Then to the nun: "Sister Teresa said we'd have a new Sister to-day and we just came to see what you were like. She's Frances Babbington and I'm Belle Sallinave—it's Isabel really, you know. And I'm foreign, too. When we heard you were from Ireland some of them thought you wouldn't know any English and that we'd have some fun."

"Please, Sister," remarked Frances *à propos* of nothing, "my great-great-grandfather was a martyr."

"An' she's going to be a nun and a martyr as well," broke in Belle, "and have her head stuck on a spike."

"And what about you?" asked the novice, smiling at the vivacious little face.

"Me? Oh! no! I'm going to be lady with pretty dresses, and then I'll get married and have some children an' they can be martyrs—that'll be better than her, won't it, Sister?"

"Sister, won't you tell us about Ireland?" entreated Frances, ignoring Belle's efforts to out-martyr her.

"It's all bogs and things, isn't it?" came the irrepressible Belle. "I'm sure it's not as nice as Spain."

"Children, children, is that where you are?" and Sister Agnes entered the room. "Up to the dormitory with you at once. You haven't touched your beds, and you know you shouldn't be here till after prayers." Then, catching Sister Augustine's eye, she smiled and said kindly: "Don't let them bother you, Sister. They're a real pair of rogues."

"I'm sorry, Sister," murmured Frances with almost suspicious meekness, and she turned obediently to follow the nun.

"I'm not," murmured Isabel, defiantly, "and I'm glad we came, too," she added as a parting shot.

At the door, Frances turned suddenly, and facing the novice and the little girl, stretched out her arms in a gesture of appeal, screwed up her face as though she were in terror, then slowly lowered her head and arms and walked sadly away.

Sister Augustine stared after her in bewilderment—was the poor child in her right mind?

" Oh, you needn't take any notice of her," said Isabel coolly. " She's playing at being a martyr captured by the king's men, and we're s'posed to be her weeping parents. Good-bye, Sister," and the little girl darted out of the door.

" What extraordinary children!" thought the nun. " I wonder if they're all like that?"

Much to her relief they were not, and the morning passed off successfully—teaching wasn't such a terrible business after all!

From that day on, Isabel and Frances claimed her as their " special " nun and were rivals for the honour of carrying her books or opening the door before her. At recreation times, too, they nearly always managed to get one on either side of her. Then, joined by the other children, they would beg for stories about Ireland—what were the girls and boys like over there? Back to her own mind would come the dear, familiar picture of Eason's Hill on a summer evening and the knot of eager listeners clustered around " dear Sean."

One afternoon Isabel asked suddenly: " Sister, when I'm twenty-one may I come to Ireland and see you?"

" Of course, you may," smiled Sister, " and I'll give you a really Irish welcome."

" Pooh," said Frances scornfully to her rival. " You couldn't do that. You wouldn't know the way."

" And couldn't I find out? I could ask someone."

" They mightn't know, an' then you'd get lost."

Isabel was nonplussed, but only for a moment.

" I'll ask—God," she said calmly. " He wouldn't let me go wrong. You'll see. I'll get there in the end." And Isabel was good as her word.

The days passed quickly. Soon their year's noviceship would be over, and then? Neither of the novices felt that she had sufficient training for the life that lay before her. After praying much for light and guidance, acting on the advice of Mother Mary Austin and of the Superior, Mother Mary Elizabeth, Sister Mary Augustine wrote to Dr. Murray asking if the two might have another year's probation. His reply, granting their request, not only brought great joy to the

Irish neophytes but also to their young companions in the noviceship, for among these they were very popular. Sister Mary Catherine carried happiness about with her because of her bright and cheerful disposition. Novices are proverbially gay, however trying their state may be, though their lightness of heart can rarely reveal itself outside of recreation. Perhaps Sister Mary Augustine was a little too grave and solemn at times. It was but natural that fears and anxieties, of which her fellow novices had no inkling, should often beset her soul.

Not indeed that she was denied those moments of consolation and light which God normally uses to woo souls to His love and service. Days there were when prayer was filled with delight, and she was acutely conscious of His presence within her; days when the longing for union with Him amounted almost to a physical pain; days when she tasted something of "the aching joys" and "dizzy raptures" of His love; but these days did not and could not last. God loved her too much to allow her to mistake His consolations for Himself. She had to learn to love Him with her will and not with tender emotions, to love Him in dryness and discouragement, to seek Him by faith and not by feeling.

"'Lord, increase my faith' must be your constant prayer," her Novice Mistress told her, when she made known her desolation of soul. She took this aspiration for her own. Faith—yes, to believe in God's love and mercy, His care and providence; to believe that in the end "all manner of things shall co-operate unto His glory." And believing this, how could she doubt? How could she fear, no matter what the future might bring?

The second year of noviceship was drawing to its close, and still Sister Mary Augustine felt unprepared for the work that lay ahead. Humanly speaking, there seemed no way of obtaining an extension, so she appealed directly to Heaven—and got her answer.

It was 1814 and all Europe was in ferment. Soon Napoleon would escape from Elba and make his last bid for Empire during the Hundred Days. Conditions were so unsettled that it was deemed wiser for the novices to make no move, especially as Dr. Murray had to go to Rome. Thus a year was to elapse before, in August, 1815, he was able to travel to York to fetch home his "dear daughters in Jesus Christ."

He had a place ready for them in North William Street, Dublin, a house which originally belonged to the Trinitarian Confraternity and had been used to shelter orphans. The president offered to hand it over to the sisters, provided that they took the orphan children with it. This they gladly agreed to do. A small chapel was added at the expense of a Miss Denis, a friend of Mrs. O'Brien. As soon as the date was fixed for the nuns to take over, a large number of pious ladies, interested in works of charity, descended on the house and subjected it to a thorough spring-clean. The poor children, fourteen in number, seemed to be in everybody's way, but they enjoyed the bustle and the new experience and rejoiced in their own way to see everything spick and span at the coming of the nuns.

It had been arranged that on August 18th they should leave York. As an immediate preparation for their new life they were to spend eight days in retreat, that in prayer and seclusion they might more fervently seek God's help and blessing. All too soon the precious days were over and Dr. Murray's presence in the convent was announced; he had arrived to bring them back to Ireland. Tears of real sorrow flowed as they took their departure. The Irish novices were dearly loved by all, while they on their part could not have anything but the liveliest feelings of gratitude towards those Loreto Sisters who had done so much to help them and whose guidance and direction they would now so sorely miss.

Dressed in secular clothes they followed Dr. Murray to the carriage. The convent door closed behind them, and from a window upstairs a dark-eyed little girl with her nose flattened against the pane, watched them sadly till they passed from view.

* * * * * *

Excitement ran high in North William Street Orphanage as thirteen little mites chatted shrilly over their supper. This consisted of thick slices of bread, covered with something that resembled butter. What a day this would be in their young lives! Oh, joy! the nuns would soon be here. Being nuns, they would be kind and gentle, and have hearts full of love and that meant everything to little people who belonged to nobody, who had never known a mother's care.

Silence fell as the missing orphan girl, who had been on the lookout for the Sisters, rushed in. From her vantage point on the stairs she could watch all that went on in the hall below and not be seen herself.

"They're here," she announced flatly, and at the tone of her voice they gazed at her open-mouthed. Something was wrong—what could it be?

"Two of them," she went on, "a tall one with a red face and a small one. An' they're not nuns at all—they're only ladies."

They were speechless with disappointment, all except Maggie, aged five, who lifted up her voice and sobbed: "Don' want any ladiesh, wantsh de nunses!"

Bar Convent, York.

CHAPTER VII

A Dream Comes True

THE SISTERS were, in actual fact, two secular ladies. A few days after their arrival from York, Dr. Murray came to visit them, when they confessed that the uncertainty of their position worried them deeply; they had no Rule, no Vows, no religious habit, no name, for officially there were as yet no Sisters of Charity. Very soon, too, they would be without a father and friend, for the Archbishop was about to leave for Rome, where he would remain for at least some months. Nothing but the most urgent business would have taken him from Dublin at a time like this, when the state of the Church in Ireland required so sorely his support and guidance. Nothing, that is, but the will of God. . . . They recognised this dashing of their hopes for what it really was, His wish that they should trust in Him alone. It only remained now to make the most of the short time available, so Dr. Murray unfolded his plan for the future.

That the Sisters might work with more freedom and security, he had decided that after a three days' retreat they should make their first vows, for one year only. That year was to be a trial one; during it they would live according to the Rule observed by the nuns at York, which was that of St. Ignatius. This appeared to be the most suitable for the future Congregation. Their chief work would consist in caring for the orphans; for the moment they would not leave the house to visit the poor. That would have to wait until they were more firmly established. For the time being it would be wiser if they attracted no outside attention, since their coming had been looked on with disfavour in many quarters. The deluge of cold water poured over every new venture had been poured abundantly over theirs, and the forecast was still showery. They would have to go carefully and give offence to none, while holding firm to their principles. Lastly, the house was to be considered a convent, and the pious ladies, to whose zeal the orphanage owed its being, were to be relieved gradually of responsibility for its maintenance. Meanwhile, they were to share the parlour and the oratory with the nuns.

* * * * * *

" Almighty and Eternal God. . . . I, Mary, in religion Sister Mary Augustine, vow to Thy Divine Majesty for one year, poverty, chastity and obedience. . . ." Her clear voice rang out in the little chapel as she pronounced the words. Her lips said " one year " but her heart added " for ever ".

" Almighty and Eternal God . . ." repeated Sister Mary Catherine.

It was September 1st, 1815, the Profession Day of the two novices Side by side they knelt at the altar rails to give themselves to God in a simple ceremony which took place during Mass. After Dr. Murray had received their vows, God gave Himself to them in Holy Communion. . . . It was a day of sheer happiness such as comes but seldom in this life, and which nothing could disturb—not even the nomination much later in the day of Sister Mary Augustine as Superior, and Sister Mary Catherine as Mistress of Novices. God was theirs now, their portion for time and eternity; they were His, and that was all that mattered. They no longer stood alone; their weakness was His strength, their powerlessness His omnipotence. Suffering and sorrow might be their portion, for were they not the spouses of Him Who died on a cross and whose very love can cause excrutiating pain, but that " peace which the world cannot give " would also be theirs, and their joy would be such as no man could take from them.

Before he set out for Rome, Dr. Murray received the first postulant, Miss Catherine Lynch of Drogheda, who entered on September 3rd. He also commissioned Father Peter Kenney, S.J., to take charge of the little community. The Sisters could have recourse to him in doubt, and as the Rule they proposed to follow was, in substance, that of the Society of Jesus, no better guide could have been found. The Archbishop and the Jesuit were united by the most intimate ties of friendship, and together they had worked, though in different spheres, for the advancement of religion and the good of their city and their country. Father Kenney immediately made the interests of the Sisters his own and was to spare neither time nor trouble in fostering within their souls a strong and virile religious spirit. Despite this new and lasting support the Sisters felt sad and desolate as they knelt to receive Dr. Murray's farewell blessing. Before he left, the kindly Archbishop had a thrilling surprise in store for them, one that he knew would afford them all the greatest consolation. They were to prepare without delay for the coming of the Guest Who would share their humble roof; the Lord of Glory was to take up His abode in their midst. The following morning, the Feast of the Nativity of Our Lady, her Divine Son took possession of His new home. There He would be the Lord and Master while its walls stood.

* * * * * *

"O Angel of God, my guardian dear," began the nun.

"O Angel iv God, me gardjin dear," chorussed the children. And the little voices went on:

> "To whom God's love commits me here.
> Ever this night be at me side,
> To light an' gar', to rule an' gui'."

Fourteen pairs of eyes regarded Mother Catherine gravely as she walked from bed to bed with her little bottle of holy water. Each child as she was blessed made a large and very solemn sign of the cross over herself, the last action of the day, to ensure a peaceful night, free from the attacks of the evil one. Then the bedclothes were gently tucked in, and with a soft "God bless you, dear child," the nun moved on. To Maggie, the "enfant terrible" of the house, she went last, partly because her bed was nearest the door, but also because there was a more elaborate ritual to be observed here. Her dolly, Mary Jane, had to have a special blessing—and sometimes to be kissed, too, while this was the time that Maggie always chose to breathe hoarse confidences into Mother Catherine's ear. To-night was no exception, and as soon as the holy water bottle was finished with, she began.

"Is hell terrible hot, mudder?"

"Oh, yes, dear, very. The fire down there never goes out."

"Then I wish I was de dibble," said the child earnestly, "for me toes is perished," and Mother Catherine, her voice choked with laughter, uncovered the little feet and rubbed them vigorously in her own warm hands till they began to glow with the heat.

" They're grand entirely now," declared Maggie, snuggling under the blankets. " Now do Mary Janeses."

" That wants a word," reminded the nun.

" Please, dear Mudder Cat'rine."

" Off to sleep with you both," she said, putting the doll into her arms, and Maggie obediently closed her eyes while Mary Jane's round black button ones stared unblinkingly at Mother Catherine as she took up her candle and moved towards the door.

" Wait till Rev. Mother hears this," she thought, as she made her way downstairs. She could picture the twinkle in her eye and hear the hearty laugh as Mother Augustine listened to her telling the story, complete with Dublin accent.

Some months had elapsed since Dr. Murray's departure. Busy months they were, for the little community was seeking to carry out his instructions as perfectly as possible, and was convinced that so much depended on this first year. Already the house had taken on quite a conventual air and the general atmosphere of recollection and prayer impressed even the casual visitor. Few there were who did not leave the convent the better for their chat with the nuns, or without being struck with admiration for their high ideals and their determination to fly in the face of convention in order to carry them out.

When Mother Catherine reached the little community room where Rev. Mother and the postulant, Sister Lynch were seated at a table on which lay a pile of children's clothes, only too obviously in need of repair, an amused smile kept playing about her lips.

" Won't you tell us the latest bed-time story?" invited Mother Augustine. Without more ado the tale was related, losing nothing in the telling, and the listeners laughed till the tears rolled down their cheeks.

" Bless the child," cried Rev. Mother, wiping her eyes. " She's surely the most original little creature. Only this morning at instruction after I had spoken to them of Our Lord in the Blessed Sacrament, I added that He was as really in the Tabernacle as truly as truly as in the stable at Bethlehem, and up she jumped and asked if the " dunkey " was in there, too!"

When the laughter that greeted this incident had subsided Rev. Mother announced gaily:

" Now, I have some news for you—guess what it is? Only three tries each," and as fast as their suggestions came tumbling out she kept shaking her head and saying: "No—no—no—not that; nowhere near it—you'd better give up."

"Please tell us, Mother," begged Sister Lynch at last.

"Indeed you should have guessed it, for you, my dear, you'll no longer be the only pebble on the beach!" Seeing the light dawn on the postulant's face, she added: "Yes, you'll shortly have some companions—and that will mean more work for the Mistress of Novices," smiling at Mother Catherine. "Please God, three or four new members are to join us soon."

"May we guess their names, Mother?"

"No, you mayn't. That's too much like counting one's chickens. You may pray for them instead—Sisters A, B, C and maybe even D," with a twinkle, for there was nothing Rev. Mother enjoyed more than a gentle teasing, and she always wished the recreations to be as happy as possible.

"But that is not all, there is something even more important," looking grave, and placing a letter on the table. "This came to-day from Rome."

"Dr. Murray!" cried Mother Catherine in joy, recognising the familiar hand. "Oh! Mother, is it good news?"

"The best," she affirmed, then opening the letter, she read:

"December 6th, 1815.

"At length, my dear child, I am enabled to write you something decisive on a matter which has been to you, most justly, for some time past, as it has been to me, a subject of deep solicitude. . . . It occurred to me . . . that the simplest and easiest way of proceeding would be to obtain for the Archbishop of Dublin a power from the Holy See to erect a congregation of Sisters of Charity, to live under his jurisdiction according to the Rules of the Convent of York . . . with the addition of a fourth vow, binding the Sisters to the peculiar duties of their state. This I have done. . . . It gives me great consolation that you and Mother Catherine are so deeply impressed with the importance of the circumstance in which you are placed. . . . You know how much depends upon the manner in which the good work is begun; and I beg of you to have constantly before your eyes, not merely the responsibility which you incur with respect to the individuals who entrust themselves to your guidance, but also the much higher responsibility which you owe to God for the success of an establishment in which His honour is so much concerned. . . . Give yourselves up into His hands, the willing but humble instruments of His goodness; and poor and miserable and powerless as you are, He will be delighted to employ you for purposes worthy of Himself. . . .

"May every blessing attend you; and believe me most sincerely, your servant in Christ,

"D. MURRAY."

Deep silence followed as the full import of the letter sank into the minds of the hearers. It was almost too good to be true. Mother Catherine mechanically watching the Rev. Mother's firm capable fingers refolding the page, thought that she must be dreaming. To be allowed vow herself to the service of the poor—it was beyond anything she had ever thought of—and raising her eyes she met the Superior's gaze, and a glance of mutual sympathy and understanding passed between them.

"Ah!" said Rev. Mother, nodding, "I know just how you feel—as if you'll wake up in a moment. When I read it for the first time I felt like that myself, and although I brought it to the chapel straight away I just couldn't say 'Thank you' to the good Lord—I could but whisper, 'Is it really true or am I only dreaming?'"

"But, Mother, it *is* a dream," cried Mother Catherine, "a dream we've both had for years, only *now* it's beginning to come true. How dreadful to wake up and find ourselves in——"

"York," supplied the Superior.

"Or Cork—or even Drogheda," added Mother Catherine, looking at the postulant who was quietly drinking in every word of the conversation.

"This is only the start," said Mother Augustine, slowly. "At present we are like the mustard seed, hidden away in the earth, but please God, we will grow and increase and provide shelter for many a poor little bird in our branches. We will do something more than care for orphans and visit the poor—we must have a school and—and a hospital—that's my real dream, a hospital!"

"A hospital!" they echoed, and Mother Catherine protested in amazement, "but, Mother, you can't do that without money!"

"And where does one usually get money, pray, but in the bank? We may not have a ha'penny in the Bank of Ireland, but there is another and a better one," and as they looked at her enquiringly: "The Bank of Divine Providence—we will open our account there, an unlimited one at that!"

"I might have known you were teasing us, Mother——"

"Never in my life was I more in earnest," came the swift denial. "It may not be for years and years, but sometime it will come; of that I feel sure, for it is God's own work. He can do it, and He will. In the meantime we will just do our little best."

And the nuns quietly put away their work as Sister Lynch went to ring the bell which brought the recreation to an end.

Before Dr. Murray returned to Dublin in March, 1816, the little community had increased by three members, Catherine Clinch, Alicia Clinch and Catherine Chamberlaine. The work had gone on apace, thanks to the additional hands. The small school originally meant for the children in the house grew daily larger as those of the neighbourhood flocked to the convent in greater numbers. When Dr. Murray visited them he expressed himself delighted with all that had happened during his absence. He was anxious to avail himself of the faculties granted by the Holy See to the Most Rev. Dr. Troy, Archbishop of Dublin, but there were many matters to be settled before the new congregation could be finally established. To Fr Kenney, therefore, he turned for advice and assistance.

On June 20th a Solemn High Mass was celebrated in the conven by Dr. Murray in honour of the Sacred Heart. In a touching sermon he explained the nature of this devotion then being introduce into Ireland for the first time. It was from the humble house in North William Street that the first sparks of that devotion were kindled which later, through confraternities and sodalities, spread so rapidl all over the country. The community looked on this privilege as ye another mark of Our Divine Lord's kindness to them, that H should have selected them, the lowliest of His spouses, to be th means of bringing the love of His Sacred Heart to God's specia favourites—the suffering poor.

On the Feast of St. Nicholas of Tolentino, September 10th, 181 Rev. Mother with Mother Catherine began to visit the poor in thei own homes. The ideal of Mary Aikenhead's early years was now reality. For the first time in Ireland nuns were seen abroad, activel engaged in the service of the sick and suffering, and people old an young gazed with wonder at the strange sight and expressed the astonishment in the outspoken manner of Dubliners. Perhaps it was because the nuns' faces were hidden by crepe veils, the people took it for granted that they could neither see nor hear, and Mother Catherine, walking demurely by her Superior's side could feel her shake with merriment as the comments reached them. Passing by a lane in the vicinity of the convent they heard one of the resident matrons calling to a neighbour:

"Biddy, run! Here's the new nuns comin'. Whist! They're stoppin' at Kitty Murphy's."

"Oh, aren't they lovely!" her friend replied. "Bill, come here, quick, run—don't wait for your coat or they'll be gone—hurry!"

"Mollie, do you see the shoes and stockin's like me poor ol' gran used to wear—God rest her soul! Did you ever see the likes of them?" and so it went on and on, while the crowd following them grew into something like a triumphal procession, and thus they were escorted back to the convent.

They did not always have such an amusing time on their rounds, and there was many and many a day when the nuns returned home sick at heart from the miseries which they were unable to relieve. If even in this modern world of slum clearance, corporation houses, municipal flats, the social service with its various ramifications, the life of a Sister of Charity "on the mission" is far from being romantic, what must it have been in those far-off days when there was no sanitation, no lighting, no heating? Even the very water had to be bought, and so could not be wasted on washing. Dirt, disease, foul smells, to say nothing of vermin, met one at every turn. Many of the children had the pinched and wizened faces of old men and women, and misshapen limbs, the legacy of years of malnutrition, and there was hardly a family, even of the better-off sort, which had not at least one member in consumption —the scourge of Ireland. If the visits of the Sisters did little to improve materially the condition of the poor, they brought, in God's Providence, an abundant spiritual harvest, but the record of those converted from lives of sin, of those consoled and comforted when in sorrow, of those brought closer to His loving heart, by the kindness, sympathy, zeal and unwearying devotion of the Sisters will be found written only in Heaven.

The year 1816 had nearly reached its close before Dr. Troy could give his attention to the canonical erection of the new Institute. At last, however, Mother Mary Augustine and Mother Mary Catherine got notice to prepare for the taking of their final vows. With the novices to join them they went into retreat at the end of November, under the direction of Fr. Kenney, S.J., who had come from Clongowes for the purpose. At an early Mass on December 9th, the two religious, having read the formula of their vows, which now included a fourth one, that of devoting their lives to the perpetual service of the poor, were thus addressed by Dr. Murray:

"I receive your Holy Vows and I admit you into the Pious Congregation of the Religious Sisters of Charity, and I promise you in the name of Our Lord Jesus Christ, Whom you have chosen for your blessed Spouse, life everlasting if you keep these Vows and the Commandments."

It was the birthday of the new Congregation—the child of Mary Aikenhead's dreams.

The Hospice, Hackney.

CHAPTER VIII

Interlude

SHORTLY BEFORE seven o'clock on a fine morning in the month of July, 1818, a carriage drew up at Portobello Harbour just outside the city boundary, on the Rathmines side of Dublin. A lady, gentleman and three nuns alighted and joined the little group of people waiting to board the covered barge or " packet " as it was called, that would soon glide away at a snail's pace towards the midlands of the Green Isle. This waterway was a favourite mode of travelling in those days, and thanks to the enterprise of the Royal and Grand Canal Companies, the general traffic through the whole country was much extended, as the principal towns of the interior were rendered easily accessible.

After some moments' delay, the gentleman, who was seeing to the tickets and the luggage, made a sign to his wife that it was time they went on board, whereupon there was a flutter among the nuns, hands were shaken, hasty good-byes whispered, and the tallest of them, disengaging herself from her Sisters, walked slowly across the short gangway on to the deck of the barge, where she stood smiling cheerfully at them, trying not to show that she was dreading the coming separation as much as they. A little distance away the horses stood waiting patiently while the tow ropes were being secured. Other last-minute preparations were quickly completed and then, when a late-comer was hurried on board, the captain's voice was heard giving the order to start. The gangway was raised, the horses walked slowly along the canal bank, the ropes tautened, lifting out of the water and the heavy barge began to move away. Farewells and good wishes were shouted and handkerchiefs waved as in wider and wider circles the eddying water swept between the travellers and the landing stage.

Mother Catherine and her novice companion stood silently watching their Mother being carried away till at last her habit was a mere blur in the distance and all that could be seen was the sparkle of her brass crucifix caught spasmodically in the sun's rays. Soon even that was no longer visible, and the Mistress of Novices, heavy at heart, turned back with the young Sister to Mrs. O'Brien's carriage which would leave them at the convent door. For the next few months the government of the little community would be in Mother Catherine's hands, and already the weight of responsibility was bearing heavily on her spirit.

"Dear, dear Lord," she prayed as the carriage went swiftly down Portobello Road, "please make her well and strong, and send her back to us soon, very, very soon," a prayer that was to be frequently on her lips during the weeks to come.

The "trial year" of 1816 had been passed with flying colours. To a great extent the criticism levelled against the new Congregation had died down, so much so that early in 1817 Dr. Murray thought it well for them to adopt a religious dress, and no longer to appear abroad as secular ladies engaged in works of charity. Accordingly, they assumed the habit so familiar to-day in Ireland and many parts of England. Outside the convent they still kept their family names, the Rev. Mother being known as "Mrs. Aikenhead," and so on for the rest. Occasionally they were mistaken for widows on account of their veils and rings. Four more postulants came to join them in the spring of that year, while in the autumn and winter they held Clothing and Profession ceremonies to which visitors were admitted, since Dr. Murray was anxious to bring the Congregation and its work to the notice of the public.

In their efforts to serve the poor, the nuns had boundless goodwill and rich stores of zeal and enthusiasm, but funds were low, far, far lower than anyone outside the convent ever guessed. At this stage their sole income came from the dowries of postulants and gifts from benefactors, and no one would have been more horrified than the pious ladies who were so genuinely interested in the welfare of the community if they knew that for quite a time, in those early years, the midday meal consisted of oatmeal porridge, with or without milk and sugar, according as the budget barometer rose and fell, and that, in the icy dampness of the Irish winter they were frequently without a fire and without bedclothes enough to keep off the cold at night. This abject poverty did not cause undue distress, or indeed any distress at all to the Sisters, who accepted their privations gladly as part of the price they were being called upon to pay in order to grow in intimacy and union with Christ Our Lord. Mother Aikenhead constantly impressed upon them that small crosses, lovingly borne, are of great value in God's sight, and it is precisely because they are so small that one hasn't even the consolation of feeling oneself heroic in bearing them. Yet these may have their place as little sacrifices offered to God, no less than the agonising desolation of the dark night of the soul, and they are free from the danger of causing spiritual pride.

Early in 1817 the first heavy cross came to the young Congregation. Some three months after her profession, Sister Mary Teresa Lynch caught fever and was soon at the point of death. Despite the efforts of the doctor she grew steadily worse. For some weeks the Rev. Mother, who had taken on the office of Infirmarian, remained up with her all night, lavishing on her all the tender treatment that a maternal heart could suggest. During the long dark hours she prayed, as only a mother can, that God might spare her child, if that were His holy will. But Sister Lynch's work was done; she died on March 14th. By then the health of another of her children was causing Mother Aikenhead anxiety. One of the novices, Sister Mary Magdalen Chamberlaine, after a heavy cold, had developed a short, hard cough. The doctor was summoned. He pronounced it to be nothing that a tonic would not remedy. The cough, however, continued, though the Sister, as novices will, declared herself to be in the best of health. There was no X-ray to prove the contrary, and it was only when she began to spit blood that Rev. Mother's suspicions were confirmed. By a special privilege, she was allowed to make her vows before God took her to Himself. Her death was another deep sorrow for the sorely-tried foundress. Next a postulant fell ill and had to be sent home, never to return, for in her case, too, the illness was to prove fatal.

While it pleased God to lessen the labourers, it pleased Him also to increase the work. During this period of stress and strain the Rev. Mother met every emergency with courage and resourcefulness. She was by turn missioner, portress, cook—and charwoman! One day when the Sisters were out she started to scrub the stairs and, with her native thoroughness, tackled the work in a businesslike manner. Habit pinned up, sleeves rolled back, well covered by a capacious apron, she was in the midst of her task and scrubbing with holy energy when there was a ring at the door. Thinking it was a tradesman, she went down as she was and opened the door to find before her—a bishop! Unperturbed, she ushered him into the parlour telling him that Rev. Mother would be along in a moment. She was as good as her word. Whether or not his lordship recognised the dignified Sister of Charity who presented herself to him soon afterwards has never been revealed. No doubt he smiled to himself, but he was far too courteous to do so openly or to make reference to the cause!

Her healthy mental constitution helped her to bear the stresses which every day increased and to meet with calm serenity the difficulties of a hitherto untrodden road. However rapidly they might multiply they could not shake her faith in the Providence of God. But nature has its limits, and though the spirit remained undaunted, the poor body finally gave way. Again the doctor had to be called, this time to the protesting Mother Superior. Her protests redoubled when she heard the verdict: for her restoration to health complete rest and change of air were necessary! Complete rest? How could she rest when there was so much to be done? Change of air? Why, that simply could not be afforded! Although the doctor held to his point, it was utterly fruitless. But the Archbishop intervened and ordered her to seek hospitality from Mrs. O'Brien who would be only too glad to receive her at her summer residence, Rahan Lodge, near Tullamore.

Hence the early morning journey to Portobello Harbour and the packet boat. With deep regret Mother Aikenhead saw herself exiled from her dear family and the things that she prized most on earth—all that was now comprised in that most precious term, her convent home. As always, however, there was not a murmur of dissent; it was "God's will," and so—"Amen!" Thus while Mother Catherine, driving home through the Dublin streets, was praying for her speedy return, Mother Aikenhead, gliding past tree-covered banks and fresh green fields, was begging God to restore her quickly to her beloved children. Mrs. O'Brien, as may well be imagined, was in her element, fussing over the dear invalid with motherly solicitude. Having seen that she was seated comfortably on the quietest part of the deck, she withdrew tactfully and went to join her husband in the cabin, knowing that it would be more restful for her nun friend to be allowed to think and pray alone.

Travelling by packet boat was nothing if not soothing to the nerves. Progress was almost imperceptible. Journeying thus was as enjoyable as a walk through the fragrant countryside, for the canal meandered through meadows and pastures and touched only the outskirts of towns and villages. In the pure air above the birds sang incessantly; down below the water gurgled and murmured as the barge moved dreamily along. In the state cabin, the flattened roof of which was really the deck, breakfast and dinner were served. The menu was invariably the same: boiled mutton and turnips cooked by the boat's " chef." Everywhere passengers sat and chatted to while away the time, and many were the acquaintances made, and the seeds of friendship sown on these delightful voyages. For the children, the locks proved a thrill, not unmixed with fear, and little ones would cling tremblingly to their mamas' skirts as the boat sank down—down—down between the stone walls of the embankment while the waters rushing through the gates threatened to engulf it. What a relief when they found themselves safe and sound on the level water once again!

Mary Aikenhead, always a lover of nature, feasted her tired eyes on the smiling countryside which, after the sordid squalor of the laneways round North William Street, was heaven indeed, and she only wished that some of her dear Sisters or children were there to enjoy it with her. How Mother Catherine, for instance, would have loved to share in her joy! The thought of her friend brought back worries, the more painful because, as yet, not confided to a single soul. It had recently become more obvious that Mother Catherine was misplaced in the important position of Mistress of Novices. Her attraction was entirely for the sick poor; though gentle, holy and delightful to live with, she lacked those intuitive qualities essential to a trainer of young religious. If justice was to be done to the future Congregation, whose very existence depended on the training given to its youthful members, Mother Catherine could not be continued in office. So much was certain; but on whom then would the work devolve? There was none upon whom the burden could be laid. In other words, it would fall on Rev. Mother herself. Yet her whole nature shrank from undertaking so responsible a task. She would need first to be taught more perfectly herself how to walk along the path of prayer before she could transmit that teaching to others. Contemplation must be the foundation on which the active life of the Sisters was to be built; a spirit of prayer must animate their works of charity and zeal, for that was the only thing that would render them really fruitful. Where was she to get the required help? Dr. Murray and Fr. Kenney had far too many demands on their time already, nor could she with propriety thrust her personal difficulties upon either. Though she turned the perplexing problem over and over in her mind she could arrive at no solution. Finally, with an act of complete trust in the Providence of God, she dropped the problem and began to say her Rosary.

Not ten yards away from where she sat was a fellow traveller who had seen her come on board and beheld her now with interest. He was a Jesuit, Fr. Robert St. Leger, the Rector of St. Stanilaus' College, Tullabeg. Having come on deck to read his breviary, he found before him the Rev. Mother of the Irish Sisters of Charity, about whom he had heard so much. Little did he realise that very soon he would be called on by Fr. Kenney to undertake the direction of her soul, and that for years to come he would guide her and her novices in the way of perfection. To address her now would have been a breach of good manners, for they had not been formally introduced, but by the time the barge reached Tullamore and they disembarked, he had seen enough to convince him that this was a woman of no ordinary quality.

During Mother Aikenhead's visit Rahan Lodge was anything but a solitude. Tullabeg College nearby and the Presentation Convent at Rahan excited much interest as new foundations of great promise, and attracted many visitors to the neighbourhood, including Dr. Murray himself. Before she was there a week, Fr. Kenney called, bringing with him Fr. St. Leger, to whom, on the former's advice, she laid open her whole soul and confided her deepest anxieties. Not the least of these was the drawing up of Constitutions which would amplify and explain the Rule. Upon them the well-being and stability of the new Congregation would mainly depend. He saw the work before him and threw his whole heart into it, first by forming the Rev. Mother herself, knowing how important it was that she should be thoroughly grounded in the whole economy of the spiritual life before she could with any degree of confidence undertake the instruction of others. He promised her his unremitting help in the training of the novices, and finally he agreed to undertake the framing of the Constitutions. A great weight was lifted off her mind.

Once again God had not failed her when things were apparently in a hopeless state.

Under Fr. St. Leger's guidance certain principles took deep root in her soul, the chief of these being confidence in God, a confidence so absolute that it gave her dauntless courage. It was at this time that she selected for her motto the words of St. Paul: "I can do all things in Him who strengthens me."

Happily, the enforced rest and fresh country air wrought a speedy change in her health. Daily, under the approving gaze of Anna Maria, she grew stronger. The colour returned to her cheeks, the sparkle to her eyes; she was her old self once more and could face, early in September, the return journey from Tullamore to Dublin.

That evening Mother Catherine, with a hymn of thanksgiving in her heart, stood again at Portobello Harbour. Away in the distance the dark shape of the incoming barge was just visible. Lovingly, she strained her eyes to catch the first glimpse of her dearest Mother.

CHAPTER IX

A Garden Enclosed

On the north side of the City of Dublin near the top of a steep hill stands an old house in a very large garden. Once it was a country residence where wealthy families, glad to escape from the dust and noise of the city, spent many a pleasant holiday. Were they to come back to-day, those ghosts of stately gentlemen, of gracious ladies, of romping boys and demure little maidens, how changed they would find it all! No longer is it surrounded by green fields traversed by country lanes; the slope beneath is now built up with very poor streets which afford a view of rows and rows of roof-tops, stretching, it would appear, almost to where the soft outline of the Dublin mountains curves like a blue cloud fringed with white along the horizon.

The district was still suburban when, in 1814, this property passed into the hands of Mrs. O'Brien, who transferred thither her House of Refuge from Ashe Street. By then it had acquired a new name, Stanhope Street. Here Mrs. O'Brien and her lady helpers continued the work they had been doing amongst the girls, training them in sewing, cookery and laundry, and enabling them thus to earn an honest livelihood. From the point of view of the girls the move was most desirable, but apart from the matron who resided with them, the ladies found the transfer inconvenient. They were bound by home ties and preferred Ashe Street, which was very central, to Stanhope Street, which was out of the way. Awkwardness increased until, in 1818, Mrs. O'Brien felt that the institution was not being cared for as it should be, and asked Mother Aikenhead to take over the entire charge. To this she gladly consented. There was, however, a difficulty, for the house was too small for nuns as well as girls, but Miss Denis again came to the rescue by providing money for the building of a chapel and cells. Thus began the second foundation of the Sisters of Charity.

It was a cold wet evening in January, 1819, and Dublin was at its dreariest when Mother Aikenhead and Sister Mary Joseph O'Reilly arrived to take possession of their new home; but on February 2nd, when Dr. Murray said Mass and blessed the house in honour of Our Lady of the Purification, the garden was filled with early spring sunlight. Some days later he nominated Mother Aikenhead Rev. Mother and Mistress of Novices in Stanhope Street, and Mother Catherine Superior in North William Street. Two professed Sisters remained on with the latter when the novices and postulants moved into the new house to join their "Mother." Almighty God, on Whom, now as always, she had so utterly relied, had settled Mother Aikenhead's worry about the noviceship and in doing so had eased Mother Catherine's position also, allowing her to heave a sigh of relief as she saw the last postulant leave. Henceforward, all her energies could be devoted without distraction to the service of the poor.

When Mother Aikenhead began her work in the novitiate she had four novices and three postulants under her care. Her own experience, derived from working on the sick mission, coupled with the warnings of Dr. Murray and Fr. Kenney, made her realise that Sisters of Charity, more than any other nuns, required a thorough training in prayer and the interior life. To give her novices this training, she tried to separate them, at least for a certain portion of their noviceship, from the secular works of the congregation, and even from mixing with the Sisters engaged therein, that the first great steps in personal sanctification might be taken without interruption or distraction. Later on, when the novices had been professed, they would have, of necessity, to "rub shoulders with the world"; they would have, indeed, to face more than the normal share of the sordid side of life. Hence the need that they should be firmly rooted and founded in the love of God. Ugly weeds in the shape of sin and misery, vice and squalor, would spring up around them once they were transplanted from the "garden enclosed" to the want and disorder of life outside, but in the midst of these they would grow and prosper if they left the noviceship radiant with spiritual health.

The mainspring of Mother Aikenhead's life and work was charity —love of God and of her neighbour. Kindness to others had become so much a part of herself, at this early stage of her religious development, that years later an old Sister, speaking of her own youthful days, could say: "The charity shown to us was just like God's own goodness," or as another yet more touchingly expressed it: " She had a heart like the Great Heart above." Mindful of the kindness shown her at York, but also of the misery and loneliness experienced by the newcomer to religion, she laid down a special code of behaviour towards postulants which has been faithfully followed from her day to this.

Noviceships are surprising places, they are so absolutely unlike anything one might imagine, but perhaps the first surprise the new postulant receives is the kindly welcome of a sincerity untainted by the least suggestion of " gush." Hardly has the door closed behind her, hardly has she blinked back the homesick tears, hardly has her mother's last kiss faded from her cheek, when a beaming novice comes to claim her and to lead her to that mysterious part of the house known as the noviceship. This novice, called her " Angel " (without wings, it is true, though a white veil makes an excellent substitute!) takes special care of her during the first bewildering week and initiates her into the routine of her new life. Not a few owe their perseverance in religion to the gracious charm and cheerfulness and the reassuring sympathy of their good angel during those first distressful days when the call of home keeps recurring with the insistent ring of an imperious telephone bell.

The major part of the novices' day was given to the study and practice of piety. Union with God was the primary aim. " No great work," Mother Aikenhead often reiterated, " was ever done for God except by persons of prayer." To transform her novices into " persons of prayer " was the chief object of her training. As an essential means to attain this she was very strict about silence and recollection. As a safeguard to words and thoughts, custody of eyes and ears was necessary. Nevertheless, even in the best regulated interiors, thoughts will wander and day dreams will occur, and it is useless to say, when the mind is in a turmoil, " Peace, be still," and expect without more ado " a great calm." Most people's minds are not vacuums; they must work on something; so Mother Aikenhead gave them that something on which to work, the acquiring of familiarity with God. " Persons of prayer " did not mean, according to her, persons who prayed for hours on their knees, but persons rather who lived a life of prayer, whose every action, no matter how trivial, was a prayer, because done for God and with God. Fidelity to Rule was a prayer because it was the "outward expression of love for Christ." Obedience was a prayer because it was the doing of His will as expressed by His representative, the Superior; and lastly, their future labours, their ceaseless, unremitting toil in the service of the poor would be prayer, since it sprang directly from love of God. In the Sister of Charity, Mary and Martha were to be united: she would serve because she loved, and through love her service would be fruitful.

Closely allied to the spirit of prayer is the spirit of penance which is a vital necessity for progress, and Mother Aikenhead's noviceship furnished opportunities for its practice in plenty. Not only did she encourage the novices to be on the look out for "the little miseries which sting self-love" that they might offer them to the suffering Christ in union with His pains, but she also never tired of impressing on them that the life of a Sister of Charity was a continual war against self and all that self stands for. The amount of self-denial entailed in the keeping of the Rules and Vows, in constant labour amid unlovely surroundings, in absence of consolation, in lack of gratitude on the part of those who were helped, these were the daily bread of a Sister of Charity. Thus nourished, the soul grows strong and self grows weak.

The love of self, "our own worst enemy," was to be replaced by the love of God, which brings with it a happiness, a peace, a contentment, a security undreamt of in the world outside. That atmosphere of joy she wished her nuns to spread wherever they went abroad. Her own heart was full of tender compassion and deep sympathy for the woes of men and women. She once asked a friend: "Did you think that I left my heart behind me when I put on the habit?" She knew that a cold, forbidding Sister of Charity would be a sorry messenger of God's love and mercy to a world steeped in sin and guilt.

Mother Aikenhead was very particular in her choice of those admitted into the Congregation. Besides a supernatural vocation, of course the essential requisite, she wished them to have heads, hands and, most of all, hearts. Heads—she wanted good sensible women, not children; women with intelligence and the knowledge and sense to use it. Hands—they must have a spirit of industry, or, as she put it with a smile: "We must not be of the tribe of the 'Mesdames Dolittle'; we have work enough on our hands everywhere"; and lastly, hearts—loving all God's creatures, especially the most abandoned, and loving them all in God.

Fr. St. Leger, true to his promise, guided Mother Aikenhead and the novices both by letter and by word of mouth, for he gave them many retreats and triduums. But by far the most telling instruction the novices received was the Mistress of Novices' example. The theory taught came to life in her, and thus she led her novices up the steep and rugged path to true sanctity.

In those early days many postulants entered, and not a few left. Some finding the noviceship standards too high and the life too hard went of their own accord, while others were considered unfitted for the works of the Congregation and were asked to find a more suitable field for their talents elsewhere.

These departures were particularly painful to Mother Aikenhead, who naturally shrank from hurting anybody. Nothing but an overwhelming sense of responsibility could overcome her repugnance when a decision of the kind had to be made. As Novice Mistress she was entrusted with the care of the " Garden Enclosed," and in that capacity owed her first duty to God. He had to be served even at the cost of offence to parents, relatives and priests who had directed young ladies to Stanhope Street, and were chagrined when their protégées were not allowed to remain.

Mother Aikenhead wished her nuns to be happy and holy. To be thus they had to " fit in "—a round peg in a square hole would be a misfit and, therefore, wrongly placed as a Sister of Charity. When she saw a postulant or novice who obviously was devoid of a spiritual outlook, or whose temperament made her a nuisance in community life, or who had not sufficient strength of character to overcome her faults, she knew that a genuine vocation was lacking and that the young person was not suitable.

Amongst those who joined the Congregation in the first days of its existence was the foundress's sister, sweet and gentle Anne Aikenhead. She was soon followed by a very gay young cousin, Mary Hennessey, who had come on a holiday to Dublin, avowedly to have a good time, but who ended up in Stanhope Street. What kind of a time she had there is not related; but, whatever it was, she had no regrets. There were also two widows, Sister M. Jerome Corbally and Sister M. de Chantal Coleman, whose delight it was to mother homesick and lonely postulants.

From 1819 until 1826 Mother Aikenhead resided at Stanhope Street, devoting herself mainly to the task of training the younger members of the Congregation, now steadily increasing. She made sure, however, while thus engaged, that the extern duties of a Sister of Charity were not neglected. A young professed Sister was placed over the House of Refuge. Novices were brought out on the sick mission by the foundress herself and taught by her the way to care for their "future family—the poor of Jesus Christ." Who, indeed, could teach this lesson as well as Mary could, for she regarded the least act of kindness to them as "direct personal service to Christ"? Instruction was given to the children in the Abbey Street School, which later was moved to King's Inns Street and finally taken over entirely by the Congregation, while visitation of Jervis Street Hospital was carried out by Sisters from North William Street. Mother Aikenhead had augmented Mother Catherine's community as soon as ever Sisters were available, thus enabling her to extend her sphere of service. Patients were visited and prepared for the Sacraments until the management of the hospital was taken over by the Sisters of Mercy. Needless to say, these were not rivals but fellow-labourers famed for their devotion to the suffering members of Christ's Body.

In 1821 the Sisters received another call, this time from Kilmainham Gaol, where two young women had been sentenced to death for murder. One of them, Bridget Ennis, was known personally to Mother Aikenhead, as her parents lived in Clarence Street and had often been visited by the nuns from North William Street. Her companion in crime was one Bridget Butterly, who till recently had been employed as a servant by a Captain Peck in Mountjoy Square. Subsequent to her dismissal she and the other Bridget had desired to go to England, but had been unable to do so far lack of money. Then one of them remembered a certain trunk in an upstairs room of her late employers. They planned a robbery. Gaining entrance to the house in the absence of the master they were surprised by the mistress. Not to be baulked in their design, they attacked and half strangled her with a scarf, and finally killed her outright with a poker. Though they escaped with the money they were soon caught and sent for trial.

Mother Aikenhead and Mother Catherine went to visit them as often as they were permitted. Thanks to the grace of God, the efforts of the prison chaplain, Fr. Lube, and the kindness and sympathy of the two nuns, the unhappy creatures were completely won over. Their former attitude of defiance was replaced by sincere sorrow for their sins. The execution was fixed for May 4th, and the Sisters were at Kilmainham at nine o'clock that morning, where they remained with the condemned pair, praying with them, consoling them and encouraging them to face the dread ordeal. At two o'clock the parting came, and the priest accompanied them to the " drop " outside the wall. There thousands of people had gathered to witness the ghastly scene. The nuns stayed a further two hours praying in the prison chapel for the departed souls of their new-found friends. From this time onwards prison visiting became one of the regular works of the congregation. Wherever souls were to be saved, there Mother Aikenhead wished her daughters to be.

With her devotion to the Sacred Heart went a very tender love for Our Blessed Lady. The longing to see her publicly honoured led to the introduction of the month of May devotions, which had never before been known in Ireland. As there was no book treating of the subject in English she procured one from Italy, had it translated and additions inserted as to the manner in which the devotions were to take place. Who could have foreseen that in acting thus she was blazing a trail that would be followed yearly by thousands and thousands of girls and boys? To-day, as through all the years that have elapsed since then, these little ones walk in the May Processions, lifting up their soft Irish voices in hymns of praise to their Heavenly Queen. But perhaps the songs dearest of all to Her Immaculate Heart were those sung one Sunday afternoon in the far-off 1820's when the first May Procession wound its way under the fresh green trees along the garden paths of a convent in Dublin.

God had bestowed on Mother Aikenhead certain gifts of character particularly suited to one who was not only called to be a foundress but also a pioneer in the service of the poor. She had, in generous measure, initiative, tact and judgment; she had a ready wit and a kindly sense of humour which often helped her on the way when the going was rough. From her father she inherited steadfastness of purpose, common sense and grit; from her mother tenderness of heart and generosity. To Mammy Rorke she owed her simple piety and her delightful familiarity with God. Her attitude towards Him was that of a child in her father's house.

She was already becoming an adept in the art of government, and

At work in the Classroom

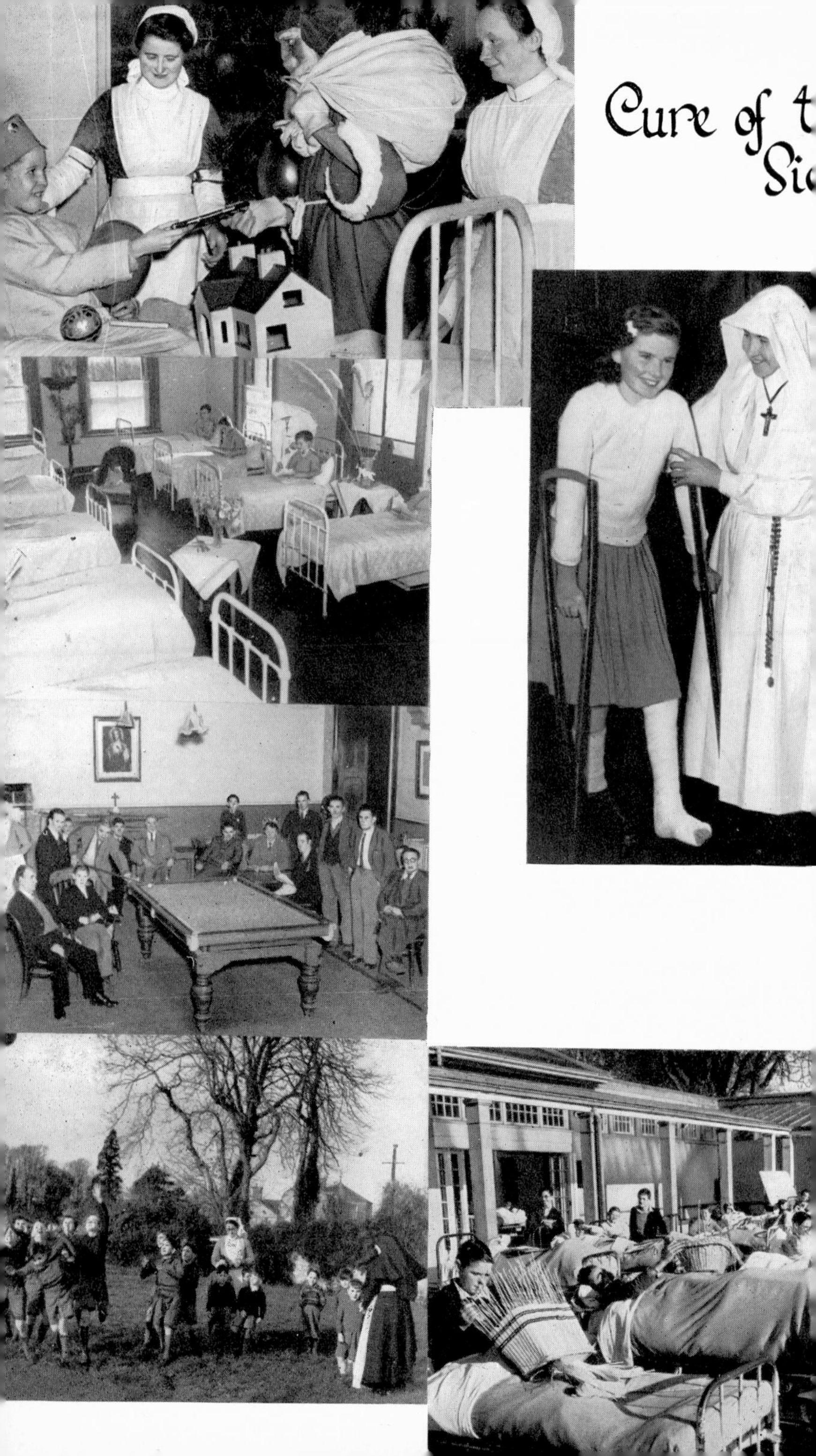
Cure of t
Sic

also in the more difficult art of administering correction, which of necessity was a part of the training of novices. Her admonitions were short and to the point and so sweet that they left no sting behind them. In fact, the faint suspicion of a twinkle in the Rev. Mother's eye gave the delinquent sure hope that all was not lost. So courage would revive and the resolution would be taken to do better in future and continue along the path that would lead to death of self and life in Christ.

CHAPTER X

A Castle in Cork

"... THEREFORE I entreat your Grace, through the Precious Blood of Jesus Christ, to look to the poor of Cork and send down a community of Sisters of Charity. . . ."

Thus ran the letter to Dr. Murray. He had forwarded it on to Mother Aikenhead, and she, holding the missive in her hand, heard once again the cry of her own townsfolk, the poor by her native Lee. It was the Bishop, Dr. Murphy, who had voiced the cry; nor was it the first time that an appeal from Cork had been made for the Sisters of Charity. As far back as 1813, before Mother Aikenhead had finished her noviceship, a certain gentleman, Timothy Mahony by name, had left a generous sum of money for the establishment of a convent there. At that time, of course, no foundation was possible, so the money had been put aside until the day when the work could be commenced. In 1824 the project was reconsidered, but once again there had been an insurmountable difficulty. Now in 1826, the third appeal had come. What was her answer to be? Her eyes rested for a moment on a little crucifix that stood close by her on the desk.

" Lord, what wouldst *Thou* have me to do?" she prayed.

" Not *my* will but *Thine* be done!"

Like a flash the decision came. The poor were calling, and that was enough! As for difficulties—well, she would leave them all in God's hands. She took up her pen and wrote.

In the autumn of that year, 1826, Dr. Murphy came to Stanhope Street. He was to bring back with him to the southern capital Mother Aikenhead and Sister Mary Regis Teeling, who would make preliminary arrangements and stay as his Lordship's guests until a house had been procured for them. On September 25th the travellers arrived at their destination, and Mother Mary saw once more, after an absence of fourteen years, the scenes of her happy childhood.

Bathed in warm sunshine and surrounded by trees still softly green but soon to be transformed into the brown fullness of autumn glory, Cork looked its best. The beauty and the dear homeliness of it nearly took her breath away—the steeples, the quays, the bridges, the sparkling river, the sights and sounds that could never cease to be an integral part of herself. She loved every nook and cranny of this dear city. No sour ascetic she, who would turn her eyes away from the splendour of created things. Rather did she accept what was good and lovely with the simple gratitude of a child, and as she eagerly pointed out familiar landmarks to her companion, the musical lilt of the famous Cork accent came from every side to charm their ears.

At the Bishop's house a little group of people waited to welcome the newcomers. Amongst them was an elderly, shy-looking man, very obviously in his Sunday-best, and, therefore, ill at ease. Once or twice he noticed the Bishop's " man " glancing at him curiously. Then he heard the whispered remarks of the maid servants behind: " 'Twas his wife that made him come, and faith she was never one to be refused!" They spoke the truth! So with quiet determination, he held his ground, despite the growing fear that maybe the grand " Mother Abbess " would fail to know him now.

" They're here!" The little group moved forward eagerly, and as the shy man was right in front, he was the first person whom Mother Aikenhead saw as she stepped from the carriage.

" Daddy John! Oh, Daddy John!" she cried, and the next instant " Little Miss Mary " was in his arms. The Bishop and his staff were entirely forgotten, and Daddy John was kissed as if Mary were still a maiden at his knee. Whatever about her " dignity and decorum," her heart was still in the right place.

The following morning Dr. Murphy brought the nuns to see the house that would be their temporary convent. He had warned them that there was nothing grand or pretentious about it, and in doing so had spoken the literal truth. It was a narrow, gloomy building, a mean house in a mean street, an eyesore that mocked at the general beauty of the city on the Lee.

" It doesn't look much now, Rev. Mother," said the Bishop, knowing well the sadness that the sight of a house so depressing must cause, " but the workmen will start on it directly, and in a month or so it should be quite in order."

" I greatly doubt it," thought Mother Aikenhead, but outwardly she nodded gravely, not trusting herself to speak lest a note of hesitation should appear in her voice.

" Now, I'll leave you to look over it yourselves," he said. Taking from his pocket the key, he opened the door. It led into a tiny, dark, musty hall. " Let me know what repairs you consider necessary, and I'll have them carried out," he added, as he went away.

" Thank you, my Lord," said the nuns respectfully. Then, exchanging glances, they started on their tour of inspection, Mother Aikenhead armed with notebook and pencil.

It was certainly a crazy structure. Its ladder-like stairs were rickety, its walls mildewed, its floor the worse for many a rotten board.

" Mice—or rats," shuddered Sister Mary Regis, indicating suspicious-looking holes in the wainscot.

" Drains, too," said the Rev. Mother, " and in very poor repair."

" Yes," came a sigh of agreement. " What a gazebo of a place!"

Mother Aikenhead's experienced eye saw how utterly unsuited the house was for a convent; its unhealthy situation and insanitary condition made it a real death-trap. It had not even the redeeming feature of a garden. But they decided to make the best of things. A hard and poor beginning would bring God's blessing on the work. Once the Sisters were established and all in working order she hoped that the Bishop would let them build, especially as a part of the money required for the purpose was already there.

By the time they had finished the inspection the list of repairs was formidable. Indeed, Sister Mary Regis proclaimed that to pull down and rebuild would be simple compared with the patching required to make the place even habitable.

" Of course," she went on to say, as her conscience reproved her for speaking uncharitably, " it may have been a nice house once!"

" Yes! once upon a time," smiled Mother Aikenhead, " so begins a fairy-tale. Once upon a time there was a castle in Cork. . . ."

" Mother, you've given it its name," declared the Sister, as they closed and locked the door. " Cork Castle, how appropriate!" They stood and took a long look at the ramshackle building. " Cork Castle," yes! Cork Castle it remained from that day forward.

In about six weeks the " Castle " was ready to be occupied. During that time many old friends called to see Mother Aikenhead, to welcome the nuns to Cork, and to offer some help in furnishing the convent. Of her own immediate family no one was now left in the city: Margaret had married a Dr. Hickson of Killarney, and the delicate brother, St. John, had not survived his twentieth year. There was one, however, whom she had to see, who was dearer to her than all friends besides, to whom, under God, she owed her faith, her piety, her love of the poor—Mammy Rorke. Tears of joy ran down the old woman's cheeks as she held in her arms once more her own "Miss Mary." Yes, it was really her own little nursling, whom she had reared and loved, scolded and watched over. Now the little one had grown into a holy nun—glory be to God, she was even a Reverend Mother! It was the answer to her years and years of humble prayer. How they talked and laughed and wept together as they recalled the past with its memories sad and gay! All too quickly this most wonderful of visits came to an end.

"We'll come soon again, Mammy," said Mother Aikenhead, as they stood up to go, "and won't you pray for us?"

"Miss Mary, alanna, haven't I been prayin' for you day and night since the first minute your poor mother, God rest her soul, put you in me arms? Look," and fumbling in the pocket of her apron, she produced her rosary, "there's the blessed beads you learnt to say your prayers on." Mother Aikenhead took the well-worn beads and gently kissed the crucifix, and in that familiar action, Mrs. Rorke saw not the "Mother Abbess from Dublin," but only a curly-headed little mite kneeling beside her at the fire and pressing her childish lips to the places "where the nails hurt poor Jesus."

On November 4th the four sisters, who were to form the community, came from Dublin. The gentle Anne, now called Sister Anne Ignatius, was one of the number. Although "Cork Castle" was cleaned and repaired, it was still dark and damp and inhabited by hordes of mice. A week later the Blessed Sacrament was deposited in the convent Oratory, and on the 19th, the Feast of St. Elizabeth of Hungary, the visitation of the poor began.

Typhus fever was raging in Cork at the time and the densely populated slum areas, wherein the Sisters worked, were hot-beds of infection, due to insufficient sanitation and want of medical attention. The misery and hunger of the poor and the appalling wretchedness of their dwellings—mere hovels for the most part—added to the magnitude of their task. The unfortunate sufferers gave them a royal welcome, for the word had gone round that it was

" Miss Mary's " nuns who were coming to visit them, and, " sure isn't she a Cork woman like ourselves. God bless her! An' didn't we all know her as an angel of charity long before they made a nun of her up in Dublin?" They did not attempt to conceal their pride in her, and they were filled with admiration and reverence for the Sisters whom they spoke of as " walking angels " and " daughters of God." Where could one find lovelier titles than these which sprang from the full hearts of the grateful poor!

During the day the Sisters on their rounds consoled and comforted the dying, while in the evenings they were kept busy preparing soup, bread and coal, which would be for those convalescent. The visitation of the sick in the North Infirmary and the instruction of penitents in St. Mary Magdalen's Asylum were also assigned to them at the Bishop's request. Quite a full programme, one might well say, but in their zeal for souls, they longed to do even more, and later took on the visitation of the South Infirmary, the teaching of catechism in the Cathedral, and evening classes for first Communicants. Adults, too, were sent to them by the clergy for instruction, and many neglected soldiers of the garrison came along to " Cork Castle " to be prepared for their first Confession and Communion, for Confirmation and Matrimony. All these ceremonies took place usually in the convent Oratory. Literally the Sisters were " rubbing shoulders with the world."

Mother Aikenhead, having set the house in order and organised the work, returned to Dublin early in 1827, leaving Sister Mary Regis as Superior. In a very short time a heavy cross was laid on the little community—Sister Mary Aloysius was stricken with typhus fever, and had barely begun to recover when Sister Anne Ignatius caught the disease. With the latter it was the beginning of the end. She fell into consumption and died a year and a half later in Stanhope Street. Henceforth the gentle Anne was to bring God's blessing on the efforts of her beloved " Mary " from her home in Heaven.

The community was soon increased by the arrival of Sister Mary de Chantal, who succeeded as Superior, when Mother Mary Regis was recalled to Dublin, and a lay Sister, who proved herself invaluable in caring for the domestic concerns of the convent, thus enabling more to be done by the Sisters on the mission.

Just as in North William Street, sickness and poverty were the two chief trials. The hardest part of their duty was patience in penury, when they had neither bite nor sup nor penny with which to relieve the hunger and cold of the suffering poor. On one occasion they started on their daily rounds with three halfpence in their purse! Kind words and prayers were all they could offer the many poor families they met that morning; while every moment their anguish of mind increased. At last they came on an evicted family sheltering in a wretched hovel. In one corner, on a heap of rags, the father lay dying, watched by his famished little children. The poor mother had gone out to beg. When the Sisters entered the children surrounded them, their pinched white faces lit up with eager eyes. Clutching little hands, too, pulled at their cloaks, while from his corner the dying man implored the nuns to do something for them. With tears of pity in their eyes, the Sisters confessed that they had no food to give, but asked the children to pray, saying that God surely would not refuse to help them in their distress.

The help came. An envelope marked " For the poor of Christ " and containing £10, was handed in to the convent. From that time forward the purse of the poor was never empty for long, since this was but the first of a series of anonymous gifts, amounting to £100 a year, and covering a period of thirty years. On another occasion, when funds were urgently needed for the relief of some destitute families, the Sisters made a strong appeal to Heaven and £50 arrived " for the suffering poor in the name of Jesus of Nazareth, King of the Jews." Twice a year this sum was sent to the nuns, nor was it till long afterwards and by the merest chance that the identity of the benefactor was discovered. He was a relative of the Bishop, Dr. Murphy.

Many other gifts of money, food, clothing and blankets found their way to the " Castle " to be distributed by the Sisters to those in need. The Cork people were nothing if not generous, and God inspired them to give when help was wanted most.

In the convent itself there was a bin which went by the name of " the miraculous bin," for its contents seemed to multiply mysteriously; no matter how much was taken from it the supply never failed.

Again in 1828 Mother Aikenhead travelled to Cork. The object of her visit was to try and get permission from his Lordship to build a regular convent, since the " Castle " continued to be both unsuitable and unhealthy. Dr. Murphy refused. He spoke most highly of the Sisters of the Congregation; they were everything that he wanted them to be. With their mode of government, however, he was not in agreement, for he preferred that the Cork community should detach itself from Dublin and be completely under his jurisdiction. In other words, he wished for diocesan rather than central government. This was the old difficulty which four years earlier had prevented the congregation from coming to Cork, and which had made Mother Aikenhead hesitate before replying to his request in 1826. Since the congregation possessed a central form of government, and since this form had been sanctioned by Rome, she found it impossible to accede to his wishes. She was convinced that in maintaining the special character of the institute, she was fulfilling God's plan and carrying out His particular design in regard to those committed to her keeping. Therefore, she stood firm. The Bishop likewise would not yield. For twenty years he withheld permission to build, so the house had to remain in its original state. During this time practically every Sister who lived at " Cork Castle " fell a victim to typhus fever; and at the end of the period the house was almost uninhabitable.

At long last relief came. The lay committee in charge of the penitentiary asked the Bishop if the entire care of St. Mary Magdalen's Asylum might be given into the hands of the nuns. He not only consented, but granted permission to build a convent on the adjoining ground. Difficulties with money, trustees and builders caused delay, and it was November, 1845, before they could move in. Even then the new home was far from ready, for men were still at work and the walls were not dry. It was, however, imperative that they should leave the " Castle," so Mother Mary de Chantal asked a doctor to give his verdict. He decided they might transfer themselves to the new building provided they occupied the top storey first. They might then, come down by degrees for, as he explained: " You have been living in a rotten house and the damp will do you no harm."

Amid great rejoicing they departed from the " Castle," and in the following June took over control of the Asylum. Five more Sisters came from Dublin to help in this new work.

Mother Aikenhead's words were beginning to come true, for she had once said: " In Cork, our Sisters seem to be the ' grain of wheat under the ground,' but with God's blessing it will one day produce its fruit."

That day was now dawning. Patience and long-suffering would, in due course, be more than rewarded. Not indeed that their troubles were over, for obstacles in plenty lay ahead, but whatever their trials, life in " Cork Castle " would no longer figure in their list.

CHAPTER XI

The Shadow of His Hand

EXCEPT for the rustle of brown paper and an occasional creak from the wicker hamper there was not a sound to be heard in the little storeroom at Stanhope Street where Mother Aikenhead was busy at work. Parcels of various sizes lay on the table before her and these she was endeavouring to pack into the basket which would travel to Cork the following day. At first it seemed as though the strawberry jam would have to be sacrificed, for the pot was an awkward shape and wouldn't fit in anywhere. But by opening the flannel and placing it flat on the bottom she discovered to her delight that the jam could now be squeezed in beside the bacon and the hamper could be closed easily. She smiled faintly as she laid a piece of paper bearing the words, " A Shrovetide party for all in Cork Castle " on top of Sister Mary Jerome's currant cake and was about to strap down the lid when the sudden jangle of a bell shattered the stillness.

Outside the hall-door was a lady, young, slender and very fashionably dressed. Her gown, with its close-fitting waist and full, slightly hooped skirt, was of dove-grey velvet, its only adornment being a double row of cherry-coloured buttons running from neck to hem. Of the same shade was the cashmere shawl draped about her shoulders. Her grey bonnet in the cottage style tied demurely with ribbons under her chin emphasised the soft darkness of her hair, which was twisted into ringlets over each ear. Eyes lustrous as pansies glowed at Mother Aikenhead, but speech had to come before the nun recognised her visitor.

" Sister Augustine," she said, " don't you know me?"

" Isabel, my dear!" and as the little Spanish lady was folded in welcoming arms, Mother Aikenhead's thoughts flew back to her noviceship days at the Bar Convent where they had first met, so long ago. " What a surprise! Where have you come from?"

" From not very far away," laughed Isabel, as she was ushered into the low, square parlour to the left of the hall. " Only from the Hibernian Hotel in Dawson Street where I'm staying with Aunt Emily. Oh, no!" as she saw the puzzled expression on the nun's face, " she's not really a relative, but I've always called her ' Aunt ' as she's my mother's dearest friend. She and Cousin Laura drove me here to-day and will call for me later. To-morrow we go to their home in Kildare, and oh, I'm so excited, I've been longing to see Ireland!"

" And I am so pleased to see you," said Mother Aikenhead warmly. " Take off your bonnet and shawl, dear, while I get you a nice cup of tea. I shan't be more than a few minutes."

" No—please, Sister," came the swift protest, " don't let's waste time in eating, there is so much to talk about," and the Reverend Mother found herself gently pulled by the sleeve on to the horsehair sofa, while Isabel found a place by her side.

" Tut, tut," chided Mother Aikenhead, disengaging herself.

" I'm sorry," Isabel laughed apologetically, " but seeing you made me quite forget that you are a Reverend Mother and that I am no longer a school girl and should act in a respectful and dignified manner—just like this," and primly smoothing her skirt she sat up very straight, joined her hands and pursed up her little mouth. " Dear Sister Augustine—Reverend Mother, I mean, I assure you I'll not offend again but will be most uncommonly well-behaved."

" Oh, no!" laughed Mother Aikenhead, " I much prefer my naughty Belle as I remember her. Now tell me how she is."

Words came tumbling out as Isabel spoke of her life at home. She told of her family, her friends, of the balls they went to, of her horse " Silverstar," of her visit to York and of the nuns there, but of the one person about whom Mother Aikenhead wished to hear—herself—she said practically nothing. At last her merry chatter came to an end. " Haven't I spoken long enough, Mother?" she asked. " Now will you please talk to me about your convent? Is this the place you told us about at school, where you had the little orphans? How jealous Elizabeth and I were of them!"

" No, dear; that was a house in North William Street, much smaller than this. It was so small, in fact, that a short time ago our Sisters moved to a larger convent in Gardiner Street. That is where Mother Catherine is now. You must call to see her on your return from Kildare."

"Yes, I'd like to very much."

"We have just opened a poor school there on an extensive scale——"

"Oh! you teach too?"

"Yes, and visit the sick and those in prison. How would you like that sort of work?"

Isabel did not reply. She appeared absorbed in contemplation of the shiny parlour floor.

"What else do you do?" she asked.

"Here we have a House of Refuge for older girls without a home of their own. They do laundry and needlework. When your aunt and cousin call for you I'll show you over it. We also have the novices here. I look after them."

Isabel raised her eyes and a spot of colour flamed in either cheek. "Do you mean you teach them how to become nuns? Is it difficult?"

"For some characters, yes; but provided a Sister is really in earnest it is wonderful what the grace of vocation can accomplish. God's help is never wanting to us if we do our part."

"I suppose not," toying with the buttons at her neck. Then after a moment: "Please," she began diffidently, "will you tell me how does one go about being a nun? That's what I've really come to ask you. . . ."

On March 19th, 1830, Isabel Sallinave arrived once more at Stanhope Street, this time to stay. The transformation of the charming little butterfly into Sister Mary Camillus, a devoted Sister of Charity, was to involve a long, hard struggle. Occasionally older Sisters would express their doubts about the new postulant. Mother Aikenhead, however, knowing well the depths that lay beneath the gay exterior, would only smile confidently and say: "Leave her to me, leave her to me."

The opening of the school at Gardiner Street was attended by great anxieties, for at first it threatened to be a hopeless failure. Mother Aikenhead, so thorough-going in everything she undertook, had fixed on Sister Mary Xavier Hennessy as the one best qualified to take charge of the new work and had given her every facility to prepare herself for the task. She had sent her and another Sister to visit all the girls' schools in and around the city. In one or other of them, she hoped, they might find a well-organised system which they could adopt. The Quaker school in Meath Street proved to be far and away the best. Mother Aikenhead engaged one of its teachers for six months to initiate the nuns into the mysteries of school management and methods; all, however, to no avail.

The children who flocked to the convent in large numbers were as wild as young goats. Most of them, fresh to school life, had little notion of discipline or obedience. Those who had been attracted to the sectarian schools by the good breakfast which was always provided as an inducement to attend, were inclined to regard all teachers with mistrust. They were a troublesome, noisy, riotous lot. Chaos reigned. Sister Mary Xavier had not the natural gifts needed to right such disorder.

The strain quickly told on her, and when Mother Aikenhead paid a visit to Gardiner Street in the early summer she was shocked at the change in her appearance. She took her aside for a long, long chat in the schoolroom, to which the odour of fresh paint still faintly clung. Sister Mary Xavier poured forth her woes and acknowledged her failure with sobs. Mother Aikenhead was all sympathy as she listened. " The fact of the matter is," Sister Xavier concluded, " I'll never make a teacher; I just can't control them. They'd need a man to subdue them."

" Very well, Sister dear," soothed the practical Reverend Mother, " we'll get a man. Why not ask the Christian Brothers for help? And once and for all put the idea out of your head that you're a disgrace to the Congregation or that I'm angry with you. How could I be displeased when you're making such a brave struggle to do God's will? He is never so near to us as when we are suffering. Don't forget that, and remember, too, that it is through the Cross that victory comes."

The idea of approaching the Christian Brothers was a happy one. On the following Sunday, Sister Mary Xavier spoke to Brother Rice, whom she met when visiting Jervis Street Hospital. To convince him that she was really in desperate straits was no easy matter, for he found it almost impossible to believe that so well-educated and gifted a Sister could have such difficulty in teaching small children. At length he agreed to help her, saying: " I'll tell you what I'll do. I'll send you Brother Duggan."

" Oh!" Dismay showed on her face as she thought of the slightly-built figure with the round childlike countenance. Why, he would never do! "Is it that—that little boy?" she faltered. "Couldn't you. . . ?"

"Little boy!" came the retort. "I wish I had fifty such little boys."

Brother Duggan appeared in the school next week and was not long in making himself master of the situation. Inserting two fingers in his mouth he emitted such a piercing whistle that the shouting mob was stunned into silence. Then, seizing a cane, he strode up and down the room brandishing it fearsomely, while the children were sorted out into their different classes and, under his eye, set to work.

Several months elapsed before the school was in anything like good order, but little by little the cloud lifted and the worried look went from Sister Mary Xavier's eyes as she and the other Sisters learnt how to exercise control and teach.

Besides his work in the classroom, Brother Duggan did the nuns another great service. He came every evening to give them lessons in the teaching of arithmetic. With his help Sister Mary Xavier compiled a "School Government Book" which dealt with every department of school life and was found to be an invaluable help by those who came after her. In course of time she became such an accomplished schoolmistress that her reputation spread beyond the boundaries of Dublin, even to England and Scotland. Often her opinion was asked for and listened to with great respect by those engaged in educational work for the poor. But for the forty years that she laboured in Gardiner Street she never forgot the kindness of the "little boy" (in mental attainment really a giant), who helped her to reap in joy what she had sown in tears. The truth of Reverend Mother's words about victory dwelling in the Cross was verified; nor was it to be in the case of Sister Xavier alone.

A shadow was already falling athwart Mother Aikenhead's own path. Much as she tried to hide the fact that she was not well, it eventually became apparent that something was seriously wrong. Mother Catherine prevailed on her to see a doctor. All were appalled when he reported that the disease was internal cancer, for which he treated her in a way that caused intense suffering. He insisted upon her taking exercise, though she found it almost impossible to walk and ordered an unsparing use of mercury, hemlock, turpentine and iodine. Not a word of complaint escaped her lips as she struggled up and down the garden paths, forcing her poor feeble body to obey

There was no improvement in her condition; rather did she become vorse. The treatment was interrupted by the apothecary who came o the nuns and said: " Ladies, you may get anyone you like to nake up these medicines. I will have nothing more to do with them. Reverend Mother is being poisoned."

At Mrs. O'Brien's suggestion Dr. Michael Joseph O'Ferrall was alled in. Prayers went up on all sides that his diagnosis might be nore favourable. It was. He declared that she was suffering from nflammation of the spine, greatly aggravated by the drastic treatment he had undergone. She would need, he said, absolute rest and ountry air if her health was to be even partially restored.

A short time previously a foundation had been made at Sandy-nount, where the Sisters visited the sick poor in the Ringsend and rishtown districts, and had started a small school. To this convent, nen, it was decided to send the sick Reverend Mother, in the hope nat the fresh sea breezes might hasten her recovery.

What passed between Mother Aikenhead's heart and that of her Divine Master during those days of trial was never revealed to any-ne, not even to her dear Mother Catherine. It was the secret of the ing, to be inviolably guarded. Never before had God asked of her ich an all-embracing sacrifice: she was being called upon to endure evere physical pain; she was conscious of becoming increasingly ependent on others; and above all, her life's work, so it seemed, as being taken from her. The care of the novices would now devolve n other shoulders. No longer would she have the joy of direct per-onal service of her beloved poor. The consolation of assisting at Iass and visiting the Blessed Sacrament would be denied her. Noth-g was left but the fulfilment of God's will, to live under the shade of His hand, outstretched caressingly," as Francis Thompson beautifully puts it, but in that, for her, lay the purpose of life self.

" Pray," she said to a Sister who sympathised with her, " that I ay make a right use of Our Lord's own prayer ' Amen,' and ask ur Heavenly Father that I may say that sweet word from my eart."

CHAPTER XII

One Morning in May

THE YEAR 1832 opened very peacefully, for the winter had been mil and spring had come early, flooding the land with sunshine. Alread though it was only March, the flowers, stirred by the soft breez gaily nodded and danced, while through the open window of h cell, in the convent garden at Sandymount, Mother Aikenhead cou hear the merry twitterings of the birds who were busy setting house in the branches of the nearby trees. Hopping about on t window-sill, eyeing her curiously, was her faithful friend, the robi Cocking his head on one side as he finished the last crumb, seemed to say: " It's good to be alive, isn't it? Why don't you co out and join us?" Then, startled by a gentle knock on the door, took flight, winging his way up and up and away into the clear sk

For the Rev. Mother, however, there was no going into the gard no rejoicing at close range in the beauty of nature. For her, life o doors was a closed book, save for the patch of sky and scudding clo that was visible from her bed. There, night and day, she lay chain powerless, inactive.

By the doctor's orders she was to keep lying down for a lo long time. Indeed, such orders were hardly needed, for the slight movement caused her intense suffering. This trial was to test, to uttermost, her patience and fortitude, coming as it did at a ti when the great public work of her Congregation was about to beg Her daughters would shortly be called upon to exhibit nothing than heroic charity in their care for the poor, while she herself, b strange irony of fate, was to remain behind the lines, a woun general. It would not be hers to lead boldly her little band in battle against disease and death. She could no longer give her lab to God and glorify Him by active service, but she could and did o in its place the homage of an uncomplaining heart.

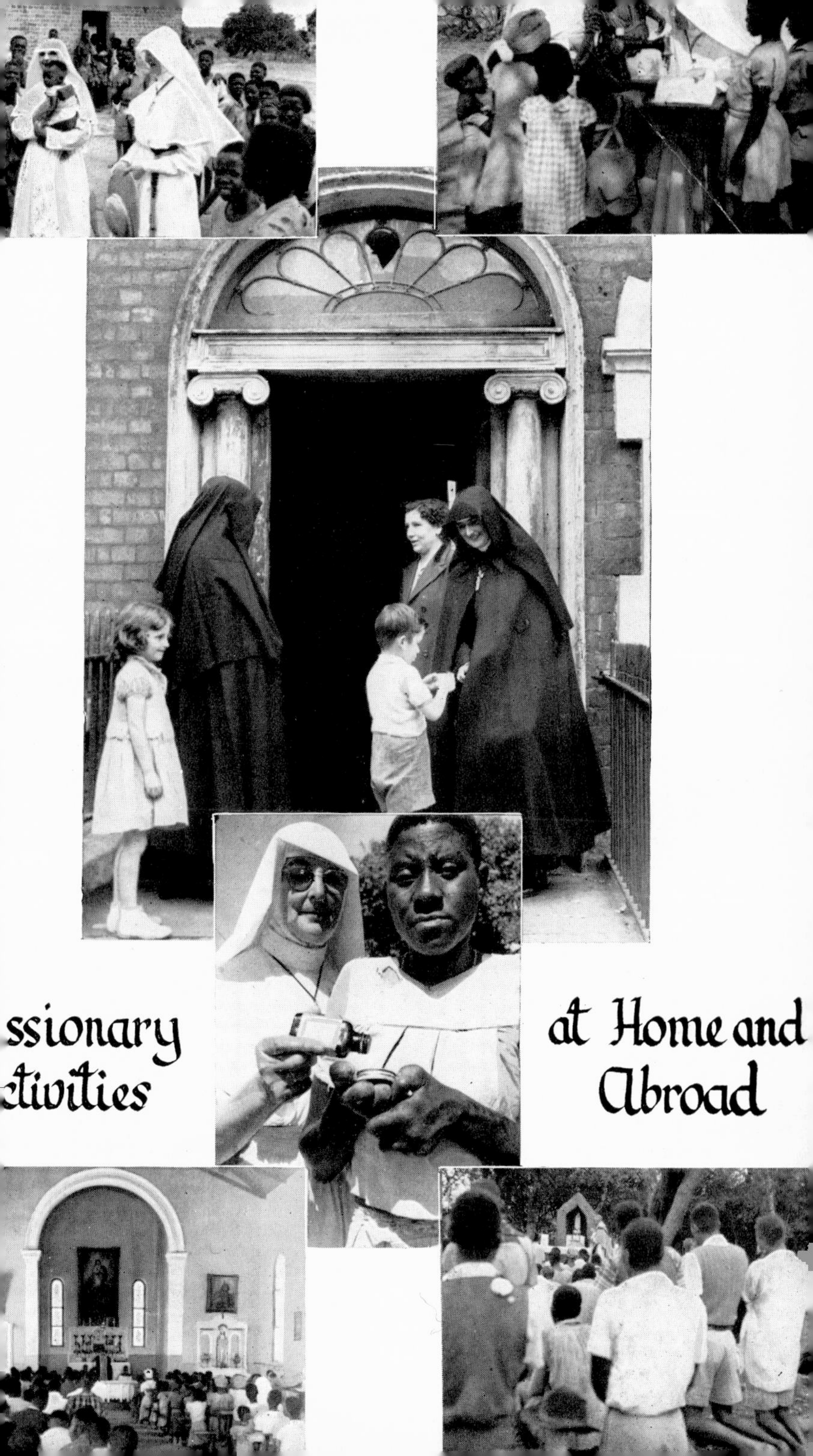

ssionary
ctivities

at Home and
Abroad

Her Spiritual Kingdom

" Come in," she called in answer to the knock that had disturbed her robin. " Well, Sister, and what is the news to-day?"

" Very bad, I'm afraid, Rev. Mother," was the reply. " The cholera seems to be spreading rapidly. The people even here in Sandymount are terror-stricken by the fearful stories that have come from Dublin. God grant that some of them may be only exaggeration. It's pitiful to see them so utterly helpless in the face of the scourge—they won't stand a chance of surviving if they stay in their wretched homes, yet what can be done for them?" Then handing her a letter she went on: " This has just come from Gardiner Street, Rev. Mother. Maybe there will be better news in it. Is there anything I can do for you?"

" Nothing, dear child, at the moment. I'm as comfortable as my old cracked spine will allow. Just say a wee prayer for those poor sufferers and for me, too, as you pass the chapel. God reward you."

Mother Aikenhead, taking the missive, felt certain that the news would not be better but rather worse, and she was right, for by this time the disease had taken firm hold on the city. It was not what was known as " simple cholera"; in its virulence and the swiftness of its attack, it was more like a plague. To go near a cholera patient was to court death. It had already ravaged India, China, Asia Minor, Russia, and, making its way through Europe, had appeared in England the previous year. Now it was Ireland's turn, and Dublin, with its densely populated slums, its overcrowded tenements, its tragic poverty, hunger and dirt, its hopelessly inadequate sanitary system, was ill-prepared to meet it. The people would die like flies—and what a death! She shivered at the thought as she slowly unfolded Mother Catherine's letter.

It was quite brief, obviously written in haste. Her worst fears were confirmed. All efforts to cure those affected were proving useless. Distressing scenes of agony were being witnessed daily. The Sisters had come across cases of sufferers expiring on straw in the midst of indescribable filth, with not even the means of procuring a drink of water. The letter concluded: " The public authorities are now seriously alarmed and within a week or two hope to convert Grangegorman Penitentiary into a cholera hospital, in an attempt to check the spread of the disease. If they are looking for volunteers to help, may we—? Oh! Mother, please say ' yes'. . . ."

" Could I ever say ' no'?" came the soft murmur. " If only I, too, might go—but what a useless old crock I am! God grant that they may do what I cannot."

Within a few days the cholera was raging from end to end of Dublin. It was a horrifying disease, for accompanying the convulsive cramps that reduced the patients to tortured wrecks, were severe attacks of vomiting and purging. The poor creatures died under unspeakably awful conditions, sometimes after only one or two hours of illness. The fact that the bodies remained warm after death or even grew warmer, and that the muscles moved spasmodically, added to the terror of the people, lest their relations, or themselves when their own time came, might be buried before they were really dead. When the emergency hospital was opened they could not be prevailed upon to go to it, preferring to die in their familiar, if filthy surroundings, than to be carried away to where the doctors were waiting, as they believed, to kill if they couldn't cure. And they could hardly be blamed for their false notions, since in those days state institutions for the relief of the poor were on a very low level indeed, as readers of Dickens will recall. As for the poor of Dublin, they knew only too well of the famous, or rather infamous, Foundling Hospital and of the so-called nurses who cared for the wretched little babies left in their charge in such a way that during a period of five years one child alone survived out of five thousand. The poor, unwanted mites succumbed to hunger, cold, neglect, or to a mysterious concoction known as " the bottle." This was administered to keep them quiet, and it succeeded. They never cried again.

In due course Archbishop Murray wrote asking that the Sisters should attend daily at the cholera hospital, not only that they might care for the bodily needs of the patients but also that their presence might " tranquillise minds suffering from the effects of both agonising disease and false terror." As Grangegorman was in the vicinity of Stanhope Street, Mother Catherine, who was to be in charge, came there to stay, and every morning at eight o'clock she and her band of volunteer nurses, some of them only novices, went to the hospital and remained on duty, with only a short interval for dinner, until nightfall.

On hearing that the nuns were at work in the hospital the poor people gradually got over their prejudice. The place filled rapidly, every portion of the extensive building being utilised. Even on the long corridors beds were ranged by the walls, leaving only a small passage in the centre.

At first the mortality was very great, averaging fifty to eighty deaths a day. Sometimes one bed had eight different occupants in the space of twenty-four hours, and the labours of the sisters consisted mainly in preparing the sufferers to meet death with cheerful resignation. The very sight of the religious habit seemed to give them confidence. The grace of the Last Sacraments brought peace to their souls, while the Crucifix held before their dying eyes was a reminder to them that they, too, no matter what their lives had been, were now at worst in the position of the good thief. And so, their cries of terror stilled, their moaning hushed, they slipped into eternity comforted in the assurance that shortly they would hear those blessed words, "Come, ye blessed of the Father, this day thou shalt be with Me in Paradise."

There was hardly a detail about the cholera hospital that was not known to Mother Aikenhead, for faithfully every week Mother Catherine's "bulletin" would arrive to give her an account of how they were progressing and to allay her fears for their safety. During the three months the epidemic lasted only one Sister caught the disease but she was back at her post in the ward quite well again after three days. Surely somebody was praying for them and her prayers were being answered in a way that was little short of miraculous.

Sometimes the notes were short enough, making very light of the difficulties, but Mother Aikenhead could read between the lines and be grieved by the realisation that the temporary hospital was lacking in every comfort and convenience. This was especially true with regard to those patients who were convalescing and who would need such careful treatment and good food to restore them to health. She also knew how very difficult it was to get reliable secular nurses, for many of those brought in to help the nuns were women of poor quality, of doubtful virtue, honesty and sobriety. To encourage themselves to face their disagreeable duties they frequently had recourse to gin, smuggled in under their shawls. They drank, too, when they got the chance, the brandy meant as a remedy for the patients and fell, because of their intemperate habits, easy victims to the disease.

The cholera had broken out in Cork also and conditions there were every bit as bad as, if not worse than, the conditions in Dublin. On reading Mother Mary de Chantal's account of their cholera hospital Mother Aikenhead, whose mind was as strong as her body was feeble, became convinced that now or never her dream of nearly eighteen years should become a reality. Her favourite occupation during those long hours when she was all alone was to pray and plan for her ideal hospital—a building large, airy, solidly comfortable, a building within whose walls the charity of Christ would reign; whose doors, like open arms, would ever hold a welcome for the sick and suffering. Her first prayer was to the Bank of Divine Providence for the necessary means—" just a few thousand, dear Lord, for a start," she would coaxingly say.

The money came as she knew it would—£3,000, the dowry of a novice. Now she could begin to plan in earnest, only waiting for an opportunity to disclose her views, and as the novice in question was a sister of Dr. O'Ferrall, it was to him she spoke first.

One morning in May he came for his usual weekly visit and after he had examined her and declared her to be slightly improved, she broached the subject.

" Doctor," she said, " if you could spare me a few moments I would be glad of your advice."

" Certainly, Rev. Mother, you know I am only too happy to be of use. I trust there is nothing the matter?"

" Oh, no, not at all," was the reply, and then, as calmly as if she were making a statement about the weather, " you know we hope to open a hospital soon."

His eyes widened in amazement. " Open a hospital! " he echoed, " but how—when—where?"

Mother Aikenhead smiled delightedly at the sensation her words had caused. It was not often that the imperturbable Dr. O'Ferrall was so taken aback.

" To answer your questions in order," ticking them off on her fingers: " How? By means of the generosity of your family." Here the doctor looked slightly embarrassed. "When? Please God, in the near future. And where? Why, that is what I want your advice about. I would like our hospital to be in a good healthy situation in a really nice neighbourhood. The building must be a large one with high, airy rooms suitable for wards, and, if possible, a ballroom or large double drawing-room that could be transformed into a chapel

A fair-sized garden at the rere would be a necessity and one in front too, or else a wide open space that would not be built upon. If there were stables or outhouses they would do very nicely for——"

"Wait a minute, Rev. Mother," protested the doctor smilingly, "why, it's not a house you want, it's a mansion! You might as well make a bid for the Earl of Meath's on St. Stephen's Green. It's up for sale I believe."

Though he spoke in jest, Mother Aikenhead replied quite seriously: "St. Stephen's Green would be just the place; it's a good locality——"

"A good locality? Why it's one of the best in Dublin! But I was only joking, Rev. Mother. You couldn't possibly have a hospital there."

"And why not, pray?"

"Well, for one excellent reason, only nobility and gentry live in those houses, and they would be sure to object to——"

"God's nobility—the suffering poor," she put in gently. "No, Doctor, on the contrary they are the very people who are going to help us. We will appeal to them to assist us and I am certain they will not refuse. Later on some of them might offer their services in caring for the patients."

He shook his head. "I'm afraid you'll never succeed in getting them to do that. Nurse the sick is the last thing anybody wants to do. You know the type of nurses they have in Grangegorman. Mrs. McAuley and her Sisters of Mercy have the same difficulty in Townsend Street. How could you expect ladies to associate with——"

"Oh, Doctor," she said earnestly, and as he looked at her flushed face and shining eyes it was impossible not to catch a spark of the enthusiasm with which she was fired, "I know that hitherto ladies would not dream of nursing because it meant working under such dreadful and dangerous conditions, but suppose in *our* hospital, with the circumstances vastly different, the nurses trained properly to care for the patients and regarded as assistants to the doctors, why, then nursing would come to be looked upon as an occupation skilled and honourable, a profession like that of medicine. True, we are setting out to do something that has never been done before but that is no reason why it shouldn't be done now."

"I wonder would it work?" he mused, and then: "What does His Grace think of all this?"

" He doesn't know—yet, but I feel confident of his approval. The next thing will be to arrange with him about getting some of our Sisters trained in nursing before we can open St. Vincent's—you see it's christened already!" Then, suddenly realising how long they'd been speaking: " Oh, Doctor, how I've delayed you; please forgive me!"

" It has been a pleasure, a real pleasure, and an inspiration too," he added under his breath, " but Rev. Mother, there's one thing you've forgotten."

" And that is?"

" To engage the services of a doctor," he said, bending over the bed and taking her hand, " and may I offer mine? Pray God I may be a credit to St. Vincent's—and to you."

Some days later Dr. Murray called rather unexpectedly and was very pleased at finding her in such good spirits and in somewhat better health. His enquiries, however, were almost brushed aside in her eagerness to tell of the conversation with Dr. O'Ferrall and to see if her plans would be approved. They were. He was genuinely delighted with her proposals and suggested that the Sisters be sent for training to a hospital in Paris belonging to nuns of the Order of St. Thomas of Villanova. He continued: " For equipment and up-to-date management it is about the best I know. If you wish I will write to the Rev. Mother to-night and find out if your plan is feasible. How many would you think of sending?"

" I'd like four to go but can only spare three who would be really suitable. It isn't everyone who has the natural qualifications necessary in a good nurse. From what I've seen, Your Grace, I am beginning to think that nurses, like teachers, are born, not made, and that to be a success in caring for the sick one must have a special attraction for that work. Do you agree or am I being over-particular?"

" On the contrary," came the reply, " in my opinion you couldn't be particular enough. This venture is an entirely new departure from the old order of things and needs a solid foundation if any lasting good is to be done. Send, therefore, those whom you consider the very best."

" Subject to your approval, Your Grace, I have already decided on Sister Mary Ignatius and Sister Mary de Sales, both well-informed, intelligent women who have shown themselves sympathetic and kindly towards the sick. The third is still a Novice but she will be professed, please God, in August. She is Sister Mary Camillus; you remember my little York friend, Isabel Sallinave?"

"The charming Spanish lady? Do you think she'll be strong enough?"

"She looks a fragile little flower but yet she has never been ill, and somehow I think the Lord wishes her to go. Every time I pray about this point she comes into my mind. It may be that she will do the greatest work of all."

"My dear child," said the Archbishop as he rose to go, "may God bless you and keep you and grant that by the time St. Vincent's is on a firm footing you may be completely cured."

"Amen, Amen, if it is His will!"

"In the meantime," he went on, "there is much to be done and much to be prayed about, so let us begin without delay."

* * * * * *

Mother Aikenhead was happy, blissfully happy, as she sat propped up in an armchair in a lofty room with a richly ornamented ceiling—a room whose windows looked on to the fashionable pleasure ground known as St. Stephen's Green. Around her knelt many of her daughters. Close beside her and sharing to the full her joy was Mother Catherine, while chief among the little group of secular friends there present was Dr. Joseph Michael O'Ferrall. At a temporary altar erected at one end of the room the Archbishop was saying Mass, offering the Holy Sacrifice for a continuance of God's blessing on their work. It was January 23rd, 1834, the birthday of St. Vincent's Hospital.

The fact that the money in hand had paid only for the purchase of the house, that there was no equipment for the hospital and that no funds were available did not trouble her in the least. She knew Him in Whom she trusted and was ready to make a magnificent act of confidence in the "Almighty Providence of Our God." He had provided. He still would provide. That was enough.

"Lord," she prayed, as the little bell tinkled thrice, "we are not worthy that Thou shouldst come under this roof. Say only the word, say only the word——"

CHAPTER XIII

A Literary Lady

MOTHER AIKENHEAD, though a shrewd judge of character, was not suspicious. As she once said herself: "Truth cannot exist in a mind that easily suspects subterfuge in others." High-minded and noble in her intercourse with those around her, she could not stoop to anything savouring of petty intrigue, to anything mean or underhand in conduct, but this very nobility of soul exposed her more than once to disappointment. There were those who did not justify her trust. At one particular period in the history of the Congregation this led to serious consequences, and havoc was wrought within the gates by the misguided zeal of one of her nuns.

It was in 1826, when Mother Aikenhead was Mistress of Novices in Stanhope Street, that she first made the acquaintance of Miss Ellet Augustine Bodenham, of Dorsetshire. She was not only a grand English lady but also an authoress with some reputation for literary ability, for she had written a book that enjoyed a wide circulation. Her letter to Mother Aikenhead, couched in rather obscure terms, asked for information about the Congregation. She gave the impression that she was writing on behalf of another person. Her queries were answered briefly. She wrote in reply and then again and again, till finally she admitted that the lady with the vocation was not a friend but herself.

Mother Aikenhead showed the letters to Father St. Leger. From the start he had misgivings; the "literary lady," he thought, would not make a good Sister of Charity, however great her prowess in the art of writing. "In her style," he said, "there is a spiritedness and playful buoyancy that is very agreeable." Apparently, however, he doubted her sincerity. Of one letter he held that "it came from one who wanted wherewith to fill a sheet of paper." Later he advised Mother Aikenhead to "recommend her to learn to knit stockings, and while doing so to reflect on St. James's doctrine of bridling the tongue."

In 1827 Miss Bodenham came to Ireland in order to meet Mother Aikenhead. On the way she went to Clongowes, where Father St. Leger interviewed her and was less impressed than ever by what he saw. It was not that he despised literary accomplishments as such —far from it—but in one who aspired to a life of labour in the service of the poor he preferred to find talents of a different kind. His view was that in the Congregation, as it then was, with its scarcity of members and increasing amount of work, " authoresses, even of *good* books, could have no place." Hands were to be put to the plough and not to the pen! In his conversation with her he put clearly before her the sacrifice such a life would entail. If she wished to show her sincerity, he said, she should begin forsaking her literary pursuits and studying how to become a practical housekeeper and needlewoman.

" But, Father," she protested, " ought not one to cultivate one's *natural* talents for the honour and glory of God? Besides, I greatly fear I am quite useless when it comes to knitting and sewing. Not ever *having* had to do anything like that makes one so dependent on others, but, of course, I am quite willing to learn if only dear Mother Aikenhead will admit me into her community. I assure you nothing could make me so happy as to be living amongst those delightful Sisters if they will only bear with a stupid poor creature like me."

" My dear young lady," the priest replied, " it seems to me your natural qualities should lead you to an order engaged in educational work rather than to the Sisters of Charity, but if you are really convinced that your call is to them, do as I suggest. Dispose yourself for religious life by the practice of humble obedience. Go now, in God's name, and we will beg Him to make known His will in your regard."

Ellet Bodenham returned to England, whence during the next few months she continued to despatch a further series of letters to Stanhope Street. In them she begged that Mother Aikenhead would at least give her a trial, promising sincerely to submit herself to her future Superiors to be moulded as they would think fit. At the same time she deplored her vanity, her weaknesses, her want of all the virtues, but asserted her determination, with God's help, to conquer her " multitude of bad habits."

Although Father St. Leger was ever ready to advise Mother Aikenhead he never pressed his opinion unduly, as he liked her to exercise to the full her own judgment. His personal disapproval of Miss Bodenham as a subject for the noviceship was not, then, a compelling reason why she should be refused admission. It was an axiom that if a prospective postulant had a supernatural motive in offering herself, was within the age limit prescribed by the Constitutions, had health sufficient to live the life and was not burthened with any worldly impediment, she was entitled to a trial. Miss Bodenham was, therefore, accepted by Mother Aikenhead. Father St. Leger continued to doubt.

On September 27th, 1827, the distinguished postulant set foot once more on Irish soil. Mother Aikenhead was at the door to welcome her when she arrived at Stanhope Street.

" Here I am, dearest Mother," Miss Bodenham exclaimed, " ready to be trained and transformed into a true Sister of Charity."

" Please God, my dear Child, and may you be very happy with us! I trust you had a pleasant journey—but what are all these?" as a multitude of boxes, trunks and packing cases began to clutter up the hall.

" Oh, just a few trifles in the way of old prints I thought you might be glad of and a selection of my favourite authors—a little variety for the convent library. Dispose of them as you think fit, dear Mother. I should be only too gratified to think this little gift of mine would help to improve the Sisters in any way."

" That is very kind of you, Ellet my dear," replied the astonished Rev. Mother. " Now, let us go to the chapel, where you can offer yourself freely and generously to God."

Ellet Bodenham knelt motionless for some minutes till a light touch on the shoulder recalled her to herself. Outside the chapel door, waiting to claim her postulant, was a merry-faced little novice with twinkling blue eyes that broke into a smile of welcome as Mother Aikenhead introduced the newcomer, adding: " She will be your good ' angel ' and will put you in on all our ways."

" Thank you, dear Rev. Mother, for your kindness," said the new postulant gratefully. " I only hope I may be worthy of it all." She turned to follow her " angel." " Oh! but I quite forgot "—she pulled erself up with a jerk—" my books; you'll take great care of them, lease, and there are one or two engravings of some value—purely entimental, of course," she added hastily.

" You may set your mind at ease, dear child. I'll see to it that hey are put in a place of safety."

In a matter of minutes Sister Bodenham, in her cell, was being lressed in her postulant's clothes, while her " cargo " of books and rints was being speedily consigned to—the attic! where it would emain untouched till the owner's religious profession, when it would ecome the property of the Congregation.

Her term of postulancy passed without a hitch and she received he Habit in the spring of the following year. The name she took was ister Mary Ignatius. So earnestly did she apply herself to the ractice of religious life that even amongst the fervent novices she vas noteworthy for her edifying behaviour. At the manual works he was exact and industrious, though it is not on record that she ver mastered the needle. Her conversation on spiritual matters was, s a fellow novice put it, " perfectly bewitching." By degrees, how- ver, it was noticed that her actions did not always tally with her rofessions. There was the time, for instance, when Mother Aiken- ead gave her permission to revise her book prior to the publication f the second edition. The occupation proved to be engrossing; so nuch indeed in accordance with her natural inclinations that she was ather slow in stopping work at the appointed time.

One evening she remained on in the noviceship after the bell had ung for evening prayer. Her " angel," seeing that she continued to vrite, came and whispered: " Sister, the bell has rung."

" The bell? Oh, yes, I heard it," and her pen continued to fly over he paper.

" But, Sister, aren't you coming? It's the prayer bell and——"

" Oh, goodness me! I suppose I must," and she rose ungraciously, igorously gathering her papers together. " Another ten minutes and hat chapter would have been finished. It's always bells, bells, bells! t's all very well when one is only sewing, but writing—that's a lifferent matter. Of course *you* would hardly understand *that*." Then, noticing the expression of surprise on the Sister's face, she dded: " And now look what you've done—made me break silence, nd I declare I was trying so hard to keep that rule," ending adroitly n a pathetic note.

Mother Aikenhead's sudden appearance at the door made explana
tions necessary. Why were they not with the other novices? Siste
Mary Ignatius, on having her fault pointed out, apologised so humbl
that no further notice was taken of the matter.

Occasionally, when she was ill, her eagerness in accepting exemp
tions from the common mode of life was very obvious. Little habit
of self-indulgence, too, were noted, but as she was never robust thes
acts were attributed to her delicate state of health and charitabl
overlooked.

On May 3rd, 1830, then having satisfied her Superiors as to he
fitness for the congregation, she was, as she expressed it, "admitte
to the honour of being a professed Sister of Charity."

That year Mother Aikenhead's health broke down. She was n
longer able to give catechetical instructions in the noviceship, so Siste
Mary Ignatius was selected to take her place, becoming at the sam
time, under the Rev. Mother's guidance, Assistant Mistress o
Novices. Nothing more was heard of her until 1833, when she wa
one of the three Sisters sent to Paris for training in hospital work
There they remained for a year. Frequent letters to Stanhope Stree
assured Mother Aikenhead of their progress. On their return fron
Paris on June 21st, 1834, the three Sisters returned to their forme
occupations, since St. Vincent's Hospital was not yet ready. Siste
Mary Ignatius thus took up duty again in the noviceship. In th
autumn Mother Aikenhead felt that the difficulties and disappoint
ments connected with St. Vincent's necessitated her own presenc
there; so she appointed Sister Mary Ignatius Rectress of Stanhop
Street and Mistress of Novices. Her " excellent temper and sisterl
charity of manner," her experience of the work, her spiritual outlook
made her, it then seemed, eminently suitable for such a position.

She was already very popular with the novices and had taken
particular interest in those who, like herself, were intellectuall
gifted. Now was her chance to plan for the betterment of the Con
gregation in their receptive minds. It mattered nothing to her tha
her ideas were totally opposed to those of Mother Aikenhead, or tha
in acting thus she was acting against authority. The novices wer
given the impression that the gifts of intellect and education many o
them possessed would never be used to the full in the Congregatio
as it had hitherto been directed. A change was needed. To work fo
the poor was very wonderful, to be sure, but it was not the only wa

in which one could serve God. One should be prepared to use one's talents to the utmost, whatever they might be, for His honour and the salvation of souls. To confine oneself to work in one direction only was to set a limit to the total amount of good done by the Congregation. . . .

Her personal charm, the great facility with which she discoursed on spiritual things, her kindly manner, won her a large following among the novices and Sisters in the community. As her schemes were carried through in a quiet, insidious way, the damage was done before Mother Aikenhead fully realised the effect of her misplaced trust. Little by little things came out which amazed her at first and then filled her with dismay. Amongst others she discovered plans were being made by Sister Mary Ignatius to open a convent at Hastings, in England, and to take there with her any of the novices who would volunteer for educational work amongst the well-to-do. Such an action, apart from the grave disobedience involved, struck at the very root of the Congregation, service of the poor, and showed quite clearly that, in entering the Sisters of Charity, Ellet Bodenham had made the mistake of her life. Her vocation was not for them, however much she desired to give her life to God in good works.

Mother Aikenhead, hoping that a change of environment would help her to make a fresh start, transferred her to Sandymount, but her ideas were already too firmly fixed and her mind continued to run on the same lines as before—she had seemingly lost all love and respect for the Congregation and its Foundress.

This state of affairs was bad enough, but worse was yet to come. At Stanhope Street many of the novices had been so strongly influenced by her " persuasive words of human wisdom " that they left the noviceship. Some Professed Sisters were also upset in their vocation, having had their confidence in Mother Aikenhead severely shaken. Two of these returned to secular life, while a third applied to Rome for permission to join another Order.

For over two years Sister Mary Ignatius remained at Sandymount, during which period Mother Aikenhead's constant prayer was that her erring daughter might come to a right understanding. " I feel for her in my heart," she wrote once, "may the Almighty touch hers. . . ."

All this time very hard things were being said about the Congregation, for Sister Mary Ignatius had many friends and sympathisers inside as well as outside the convent who considered her the victim of unjust treatment. In the interests of peace and charity Mother Aikenhead was obliged to remain silent, but in 1837 matters had reached such a pitch that she knew a decisive step must be taken and the axe laid to the root of the trouble, or the very life of her Congregation would soon be threatened.

She put the case before Dr. Murray and received leave to dismiss the offender. So one day the former Miss Bodenham left the convent and the shores of Ireland, landing eventually in France, where she decided to try her vocation once more.

All through this trial, which was one of indescribable anguish, Mother Aikenhead acted with amazing self-control. Not a word of complaint or unkindness ever fell from her lips. Not a hint was dropped that savoured of self-defence. This cross came from God. She prayed and begged others to pray that she might accept it with humble patience, that she might never do or say anything that would offend Him. Above all she pleaded for prayers that the poor soul who was the cause of her pain might be touched by grace. She never once condemned her or permitted others to do so. She wrote when the trouble was at its height: "He Who sees all can alone judge; therefore let our cause be committed to Him alone."

When her burden seemed almost too heavy to bear, a visit to the Blessed Sacrament restored her confidence and courage. God was her only hope; she knew that He would never fail her.

By degrees peace was restored and her patience rewarded. From that time onwards attachment to the Superior and loyalty to the Institute became a characteristic of her Congregation. To those who remained faithful she was more than ever "The Mother." It was the fruit of her bitter sufferings.

And what was the end of the Sister who had caused such trouble? She left the French convent before profession and thereafter led a restless, unsettled life, oscillating between England and France. Eventually she joined the Canonesses of the Royal Chapter of St. Anne of Munich, established at Tours. This was a congregation of secular ladies engaged in apostolic works of divers kinds, and none but " descendants of ancient Catholic families with unblemished escutcheons could be received therein." Here, after her storm-tossed life of brilliant promise unfulfilled, did she find " peace at the last " and, it is to be hoped, happiness also, for in spite of her many fruitless wanderings her end was in fidelity to God.

King's Inn Street Schools, Dublin.

CHAPTER XIV

The Child of Her Heart

TWELVE BEDS, two nursing sisters and one doctor, that was how i began; but as Sister Mary Camillus, candle in hand, stole softl through the ward, she felt as proud as if she were going the round in the great Paris hospital itself. She had reason, indeed, for he pride, for the French hospital was only one of many liberall financed by the Government of the country, while St. Vincent' lacked almost everything that from a worldly point of view goes t make for success. Money, sympathy, the support of those in power– all these were wanting, and it needed more than ordinary courage o Mother Aikenhead's part to start her hospital at such a time.

Though emancipation had been won in 1829 the Catholics c Ireland were still, as a body, timid, spiritless, dejected, unenthusiasti for new undertakings. They were conscious of yesterday's serfdom excluded from positions of trust. The public hospitals, the school of medicine, surgery and law were all under non-Catholic contro St. Vincent's, therefore, which had that day thrown open its door to the poor, was not merely a home in which a handful of sick an suffering bodies were nursed back to health, but a portent and symbol as well. Just as the first snowdrop, bravely pushing its wa through the dark earth, comes as a sign that Winter is past, so t the Catholic poor of Dublin the advent of St. Vincent's Hospit was a sign that the Springtime of better days was coming soo Their hearts, so long deprived of love, would feel the kindnes sympathy and tender care that awaited them within its walls.

Shielding the flame with her cupped hand, Sister Mary Camill moved from bed to bed anxious to see that every patient was settle comfortably for the night before she went off duty. Only the clin of a cinder falling from the grate, an odd snore and the heav breathing of the sleeping, disturbed the stillness of the ward. One two were yet awake and welcomed her with a happy nod that bespol content; while old Granny Donnelly, brave and smiling always though crippled with rheumatism, whispered her thanks in the delightful words: " Sheets an' blankets an' a bed to meself an' all—I never seen the like of it before! God bless the nuns!"

" And God bless you too," came the soft response.

" Sister!" a muffled sob came from the bed in the corner.

" Mrs. O'Leary—awake still and crying too!" going over to her. " Why, what *is* the matter? Is the pain bad?"

" No, Sister, 'tis not the pain at all, but I'm that worried I just can't sleep," and the tears ran down the poor wan cheeks. " O dear God, what will I do?"

Placing her candle on the floor, Sister Mary Camillus knelt beside the bed and, putting her arms about the heaving shoulders, asked gently: " Won't you tell me what's the matter? Maybe I could help you," and bit by bit the woman's story came out. Even the telling of it seemed to relieve her, for her sobs gradually subsided to an occasional dry choke as she listened, calmly enough, to the comforting words of the nun.

" You believe God loves you, don't you?"

A nod.

" And that He loves your children too?"

Another nod while her eyes threatened tears again.

" Well, then, won't you trust them to His loving care? If you will only do that He will see to everything else. I know He will—but you mustn't doubt. We hurt Him when we doubt. But you are going to trust Him, aren't you?" she pleaded earnestly.

" I'll try," replied the sick woman slowly.

" Then I promise you they'll come to no harm, but you must show you trust Him by not fretting—and no more tears," she added kindly, rising to her feet and turning the damp pillow; " and now here's a nice drink."

Nonie O'Leary took it gratefully, for she suffered from parching thirst. " O Sister," she said, " you're an angel, a real angel."

" I don't know so much about that," smiled the nun. " That's better, isn't it?" taking the cup. " Now, down you go under the clothes, and mind, not another worry!" as she tucked the blankets in around her.

" Close your eyes"—Nonie obediently shut them—" and say this little prayer after me: ' O Sacred Heart of Jesus I place all my trust in Thee'," and to Mrs. O'Leary those familiar words held to-night a new meaning.

"Off to sleep with you now," came a final whisper, and the last sound she heard was the rustle of a white apron as Sister moved down the ward.

As she closed the door behind her the candle guttered for a moment in the draught and Sister Mary Camillus shivered slightly, less from the cold than from apprehension as she began the long climb to where the nuns' quarters were, at the top of the house. Though a courageous little soul and a strong character there lurked at the bottom of her heart two fears shared in common with many of the women of her day and, indeed, with women of all times. One was fear of the dark and the other the fear of mice. And the no-man's land between the ward and the convent held dreadful possibilities of either or both! By day it was peopled by workmen—bluff, honest fellows who whistled and chaffed one another when the nuns were out of earshot; but by night! Who could tell what shades from the other world had possession of it then! Did they come back, those lords and ladies of bygone days when Dublin was second only to London as a city of brilliant social life? Did they come back, those ghosts, to haunt this house which night after night had re-echoed with music and laughter? Why, the very staircase which she trod had once resounded with the patter of little feet—little feet that had danced their way through life and now would dance no more. Unless . . . but no! Her own little feet were all she could hear, and the beating of her heart, as she swiftly mounted up and up, pausing only for breath at the landings where the empty rooms, black gaping voids beyond the range of her candle, held nameless terrors. At last she reached the top and, turning round the corner, saw with thanksgiving a flood of light streaming from the half-open door of Mother Aikenhead's cell.

"Come along in!" came a cheerful call. "I've been listening out for you this age. Is Sister Francis Magdalen coming too?"

"She'll be up in a few minutes, Mother," replied Sister Mary Camillus, entering the room, where Mother Aikenhead, sitting up in bed, was busily putting the last few stitches in a pillow case. "I left her giving directions to the night nurse. Up to a few hours ago Dr. O'Ferrall was afraid he wouldn't be able to get anybody, but then he thought of Mrs. Reidy, one of his former patients. She seems a kind, reliable sort of woman and, poor thing, she's delighted to get the money as her husband is out of work."

"Thank God we are the means of giving her employment. Perhaps we could help her husband too. There's plenty a handy man could do around the hospital. You must find out about him to-morrow, Sister; and now sit down and tell me everything right from the start."

Sister Mary Camillus, glad to be encouraged, plunged into an account of the day's happenings—how Sister Francis Magdalen and herself barely had time to put the finishing touches to the ward when their first patient arrived; how Dr. O'Ferrall brought most of them to the hospital in his own carriage; how they had welcomed them and tried to make them feel at home; all this and much more was poured into the Rev. Mother's delighted ear, for not the smallest detail was without interest for her.

"And, Mother," concluded Sister Mary Camillus in triumph, "we have twenty-five more applications."

"Splendid! Now we must hurry with the next two wards. That's been a great day's work, thank God. You're sure they're all happy and comfortable?"

"All but one," came the slow reply, "but she'll be happy, too, once you've heard about it, Mother." Looking quickly at her in the soft glow of the lamp, Mother Aikenhead could see the dark eyes of little Belle Sallinave pleadingly fixed on her, just as they used to be in the convent at York when the child tried to coax one of her friends off punishment. "It's a story *you* won't be able to resist."

"Hm—so I'm to do something, am I? Well, then, let's hear about it."

Sister Mary Camillus leaned forward, her small hands resting on her knees, and with breathless eagerness, began her story.

"It's Mrs. Nonie O'Leary, a widow with three children; the eldest is only eleven. She's been suffering several years from internal cancer and the doctor holds little hope of her recovery."

"Poor, poor creature," interposed Mother Aikenhead pityingly. "Does she know herself how bad she is?"

"I think so, because she's worrying terribly about what will happen the children when she is gone. I found her crying bitterly, and, oh, Mother, my heart just went out to her, she seemed so forlorn. Apparently none of her husband's people will take the children, and she hasn't seen any of her own family since she left home over twenty years ago. She came originally from a place called Ballingeary."

"West Cork! I know it well, but Sister, what did you say to comfort her? Did you tell her we'd help her?"

Sister Mary Camillus lowered her eyes and said demurely: "I told her to put all her trust in God and that everything would be all right because I—I knew——"

"Yes?" prompted Mother Aikenhead.

"Because I knew He would help her through—through you—for you never refuse anybody anything, dear Rev. Mother," and the laughing eyes were raised once more to meet their Mother's kindly glance. "Now what may I tell her?"

"Tell her," said Mother Aikenhead deliberately, "that she need have no more anxiety, her children will be ours. We will make arrangements to have them taken at Stanhope Street as soon as she wishes. Now, my heart, is that what you want?"

"Just that," was the emphatic response. "Thank you, dear, dear Mother. I'll get her to pray for you."

"Do my dear child; I need prayers badly. And you, be sure you thank Our Lord for giving you the chance of bringing comfort to that poor soul. I always count it one of my greatest blessings when I can be of help to someone, even in the smallest way."

"Yes, Mother, I shall do that. And won't she be happy in the morning when——" she stopped. In her mind she saw the sobbing figure of Nonie O'Leary eating her heart out during the long hours of the night . . . she saw, too, the staircase, dark and cold. . . . She hesitated, but only for a moment, then said in a low voice that sounded strangely unlike her own: "I'll tell her—now, Mother, if I may." She picked up her candle and vanished before the Rev. Mother realised what she was about.

"A Sister of Charity after my own heart," murmured Mother Aikenhead as she listened to her retreating footsteps. "O Lord, send me many more like her," and looking at the large picture of the head of Christ that hung on the wall opposite her bed: "Thank You for all the graces of this day."

The clock on the mantelshelf showed her it still wanted a few minutes to nine. There would be just time for the last couple of stitches, so she picked up the pillow slip once more. As her needle flashed busily her thoughts went back over the fifteen or so weary months that had elapsed since Archbishop Murray had said the first Mass in St. Vincent's Hospital and given the house his blessing. Right from the very start there had been upsets and disappointments, the greatest of all, apart from the trouble with Sister Mary Ignatius, being the coldness and lack of encouragement from the people whom she had believed to be friends and well-wishers. She had appealed for subscriptions, Dublin had turned a deaf ear. She had then got out a prospectus, begging in the name of Christ for help, and had copies circulated everywhere in and around the city. A small response was the result, but at least it was a beginning, and so she held firmly to her purpose.

There had been difficulty about the building, too, for though the house was in good repair, certain alterations had to be made, and the chief of these was, at the Archbishop's request, the raising of the roof so that the attics could be transformed into suitable convent premises for the community.

To bring a blessing on the work she had taken in four patients privately, long before the day when the open door of St. Joseph's ward and the twelve white beds within gave proof that St. Vincent's Hospital was a reality, though as yet she could not count on £20 a year for its support.

Nonie O'Leary lay staring, dry-eyed and sleepless, at the flickering firelight on the ceiling.

"I trust in Thee," she murmured, "O Sacred Heart——"

"Still awake?" came a gentle voice. "I have good news for you, so cheer up now. Our Rev. Mother says you're not to worry—your little ones will be ours, and we will take care of them for you."

Nonie's eyes fairly shone their gratitude and for a moment the sunken cheeks lost their pallor. She would have poured out a flood of thanks had not Sister Mary Camillus held up a protesting finger.

"Hush! don't thank me; it's our Rev. Mother who's doing it, and I want you to pray for her. She's an invalid at present and we would be so happy if God would give her back even a little strength so that she might be able to come down and see you all. You will remember her, won't you?"

"Indeed, yes. I couldn't forget such kindness. I'll pray for her now and when——"

She paused and the nun nodded understandingly.

" Yes, she will be so grateful. And when the patients have Mother Mary Aikenhead down to visit them I'll say——"

" Aikenhead," broke in Nonie with a puzzled look. " Aikenhead, Miss Mary Aikenhead. I seem——"

" No, not ' Miss '," came the smiling correction. " It's ' Mother,' Mother Mary Aikenhead. Do you know her?"

" I seem to know the name, but yet I just can't say where I've heard it—Aikenhead, Mary Aikenhead."

" You'll probably remember to-morrow. God bless you, dear, and happy dreams!"

The sick woman's radiant smile was more than reward enough for Sister Mary Camillus as she bravely faced the darkness once again.

Five days later Nonie was in her grave. Though she racked her memory during those days she died without recalling an incident in Cork over a quarter of a century ago. It had happened one night when as a little maid, newly come to service, she had peered over a balcony enthralled by a brilliant scene below and had been captivated by the charm of a gallant gentleman and impressed by the story of a certain young lady with a lavender sash, who wished to give her life and her love to none but God Himself.

By the end of the first year the patients numbered forty, for a second and third ward had been opened, not to mention a ward for children. More Sisters came to join the two pioneers. Their number needed a further increase when early in 1836 St. Patrick's ward for men was opened, bringing the total number of beds to sixty. A second doctor, O'Bryen Bellingham, was added to the staff. A consulting room, bathroom, post-mortem room and a pharmacy completed the work, and as there was no more space for expansion, the hospital remained thus till 1841, when the adjoining house, the property of the Marquess of Westmeath, was purchased.

In the meantime, Sister Francis Magdalen was appointed Superior, or " Mother Rectress " as she was called, in contradistinction to Mother Aikenhead who was known as " Rev. Mother." Sister Mary Camillus, who was a born organiser and had thoroughly mastered the whole system of the Parisian hospital, soon had St. Vincent's running smoothly. She spared no pains in teaching the younger Sisters how to care for the sick. No better person could have been chosen to set a headline for those who would come after, and to transmit the spirit of the Foundress—the spirit of faith and love—to the future generations of nursing Sisters.

That the poor of Christ might receive from their hands what the rich could buy with money was the oft expressed wish of Mother Aikenhead. She wanted also the patients to be happy. Her hospital was to be as " homely " as love could make it. She herself was the Mother, keeping an ever-watchful eye over the development of what has fittingly been called " the child of her heart." Even more fittingly could it be called " the child of her prayer and suffering—the fruit of her pain," all the dearer because it cost her so much.

The improvement in her health which had begun at Sandymount continued. There were days when, aided by a stick, she could make a slow and painful descent of the stairs, walk through the wards, and receive visitors in the parlour. When she was unable to leave her room these had to face the long climb up. Possibly strangers were not a little surprised when they reached the attics to find themselves in a spacious, lightsome, airy region. The corridor opened into a little hall floored with black and white tiles, while a statue of Our Lady, with a pot of myrtle or fuchsia before it, occupied a prominent position at one side. A door from this vestibule led into the Rev. Mother's sitting-room which, together with the adjoining cell, formed the boundary beyond which she did not pass for days, weeks and even months together. There she suffered countless pains; there she planned great things; from there her motherly influence radiated over the whole hospital, from the oldest patient to the latest arrival. Whatever happened within or without, she had one great joy as she retired to rest each night—she knew that under the same roof with herself were God's afflicted creatures, and that of the fifty or sixty sick or hurt who were settled for the night in the Earl of Meath's drawing-rooms, there was not one who would not be the better in body or soul for the sojourn in St. Vincent's.

Mother Aikenhead never lost her love for children, so theirs was pre-eminently her favourite ward. When she was up and about her daily visit to them was never omitted. The tap-tap-tap of her stick, heralding her approach, was a welcome signal to the little sufferers. Her capacious pockets, filled with surprises, would rapidly empty as she moved from bed to bed, coaxing smiles into tired little faces or changing tears into laughter. It was on a small boy from this ward that the first operation was performed; surely a landmark in the life of any hospital.

Surgical practice at this date was very limited, for anæsthetics had not yet been introduced, nor was there any means of preventing sepsis. None but the most skilful men applied the technique, which was only used in cases of absolute necessity, such as in the treatment of abscess, removal of superficial tumours, amputations, blood-letting and a few other specialised cases. A Dublin doctor has left on record a vivid picture of what was the common experience of surgeons in those days:—

> "When anæsthetics were unknown," he writes, "patients had always to be held, often strapped down to the table while operations proceeded, and the groans and screams, especially in the case of women and children, were most distressing to hear. Instead of the deliberate care with which operations are now performed, surgeons vied with each other as to which would perform an operation in the shortest time. Much blood was lost. A tourniquet would be applied were a limb to be amputated, but beyond this no attempt would be made to temporarily arrest hæmorrhage; the bone being sawn through, then the arteries would be ligatured with silk and the stump dressed."

One shudders at the crudity of such statements, and can well understand how operations must have been dreaded by patients and doctors alike.

Daniel O'Connell, the bearer of a famous name but of a feeble, undersized little body, was the first sufferer in St. Vincent's to face the surgeon's knife. A typical child of the Dublin streets with his white peaked face and mop of unruly dark hair, he came in with a painful abscess on his right leg. Poultices failed, the trouble was too deep-seated; so Dr. O'Ferrall came to the momentous decision that an operation would be necessary. The abscess would have to be lanced. When the word was brought to Mother Aikenhead she said quietly: "I couldn't have that child strapped to any table. I'll hold him on my lap." So Danny was wrapped in a shawl, lifted bodily from his bed and carried to a small room off the ward where Mother Aikenhead was seated.

" Me leg hurts," he whimpered, as he was placed on her knee, his lower lip pathetically drooping.

" Poor Danny," said the Rev. Mother soothingly, as she brushed a lock of hair away from his eyes. " Wouldn't you like an apple?"

" Yes."

" Please," prompted Sister Mary Camillus.

" And here's a sweetie, too," diving again into her pocket. " You'd like that as well, wouldn't you?"

" Yes "—and after a pause—" please."

" Good boy," nodded Mother Aikenhead approvingly, as she watched him examine the fruit, smell it and then dig his teeth into the reddest part. After a few minutes' silence, broken only by the sound of munching, he looked up and noticed Dr. O'Ferrall standing by the door.

" I don't like that man," he declared. " He's goin' to stick a knife in me."

" Is he? How do you know?"

" I heard him tellin' Sister 'Millus yesterday that he'd have to use a knife on me, an' I tell you, I don't like him."

" Look, here comes pussy," said Mother Aikenhead as the cat stalked in on her morning tour of the house. " Puss, puss, puss!" called the child, but puss knew better than to go within reach of the eager, outstretched hand. Instead she picked her steps daintily over to the doctor, and with arched back and tail erect, she rubbed herself ingratiatingly against his trouser leg, purring contentedly the while.

" Pussy thinks he's a nice man. She likes the doctor, Danny. See, she's not afraid of him."

" Hm," the reply was non-committal. " Will he cut *her* up, too?" Then a thought struck his fertile little brain. " I nivver seen the inside of a cat," he began, coaxingly and confidingly looking up into the Rev. Mother's face, " but me brother once brought home a dog that was killed. A carriage wheel went over him just here," indicating the exact spot on his own person. " He was squez flat, he was, an' was hard an' cold, an' I was sorry, an' I was goin' to bring him to bed wif me to make him warm agin but me mother——"

" Danny," Mother Aikenhead tried to hide the smile that twinkled in her eyes and played about the corners of her mouth as she cut short his gruesome reminiscences, " now I'll tell you story."

" Ooh!" and he wriggled in anticipation.

" Lean right back against me, yes, that's it," and she pillowed th dark head against her breast, encircling the thin little body wit protecting arms. " It's the story of a boy named Jesus——"

" You touldt us that one before," interrupted Danny. " He was good boy—tell me now about a bad 'un, a fella like me that throw stones. Me father sez I need a good skelpin'!"

" Very well, then, but you must shut your eyes up tight and the you'll see all the things I'll tell you about." Softly and very, ver slowly she began:

" Once upon a time, long, long ago there was a little bird wh built her nest at the top of a very high tree, the highest tree in th whole world, for she said to herself, ' No naughty boy will ever fin my nest or rob me of my eggs.' Well, one fine day who came int the wood but a bad, bold boy named John——"

" Danny," came the muffled correction, and a sleepy eye wa cocked at her.

" Danny," she amended, " and Danny saw that little bird's ne high up at the top of the tree and he started to climb up to it. U and up he went through the green leaves till he could no longe see the earth beneath. Then the wind began to blow, puff, puff, puf and the branches swayed to and fro, to and fro, just like this," an she started to rock gently backwards and forwards, murmurin softly, " to and fro, to and fro, and Danny on the branch swaye to and fro. . . ." Her voice sank to a soft whisper, then she rocke him a little while in silence till thud! the apple fell to the floo unheeded. Danny was asleep.

She gave a sign to Sister Mary Camillus who gently slipped clean towel under the poor sore leg, and Dr. O'Ferrall waited, kni in hand. He paused a moment before moving forward. To him th little scene presented a picture symbolic of the very purpose Mother Aikenhead's life. For though she held but one little bo in her arms, he was an image of the whole humanity, sick an suffering, waiting to be comforted. Her desire to bring relief wa boundless; it knew no limit but that of God's will.

He bent over the child and firmly but gently took the foot in h left hand. Danny stirred uneasily. Mother Aikenhead gathered hi loser to her heart. In a few seconds the healing wound would be nade. Her dear little " desperado," his happy dreams dispelled, vould wake, screaming with pain, to the world of reality. His pain vould be hers also. . . . He would lie writhing in her arms. A ump of pity rose in her throat, and it was through a mist she saw he knife poise for an instant over the red and angry abscess, then wiftly plunge down making a clean incision.

Mother Mary Aikenhead in her wheelchair.

CHAPTER XV

Beneath the Southern Cross

ON THE last day of the year 1838 a merchant vessel, the *Sir Franci Spaight,* after a storm-tossed journey of four months, droppe anchor in the deep-blue waters of Sydney Harbour. Standing on th deck, eagerly gazing at the land that was to be their new home were five Sisters of Charity, and though their first glimpse of i under the sparkling mid-summer sun was fair indeed, the thought of all must surely have winged their way back over the miles an miles of heaving water that now lay between them and the Emerald Isle of their birth.

They noticed the wharf black with people who, they supposed had come to meet relatives or friends, and for an instant they fel terribly alone. In all that throng there was not one familiar face with hearts, therefore, that sank, they moved slowly towards th gangway.

"God bless you, ladies, and good luck!" said a sailor standin by. Then from the crowd there rose a sudden shout, followed b the cry: "Welcome! Welcome!"

"Sisters," said Dr. Ullathorne, who was standing just behin them, "wave to the people. They're calling to you," and he himsel raised his hat in salutation. The nuns, astonished, rather shyl obeyed; and so it was amid rousing cheers that the Sisters first se foot on Australian shores. They were not landing among stranger but among friends.

Some days later a public meeting was held, not only to welcom back Dr. Ullathorne, the beloved Vicar-General of the diocese, wh had been in Europe seeking help for his mission, but also to gree the priests and nuns who had responded to his appeal and wh were come to spend their lives in the service of the Church i Australia. In a touching little speech about the consecrated lives o the Sisters, he summed up their vocation by saying that in this lan o which they had now come they saw "the Cross lifted up and Christ upon it in bitter suffering. Like the Marys of old, they hirsted to be near Him in His agony. Wherever human miseries ıre greatest there also will they be found. They will seek the bruised; hey will bind up the broken heart; they will pour oil and wine and ›alm—the oil of mercy, the wine of charity, the balm of heavenly :onsolation."

These hopes and prophecies were accomplished to the very letter, ›ut it was not amongst the poor of Sydney the Sisters of Charity ›egan their labours. At first they went to what was probably the nost forsaken and desolate post of the mission field—the convict ettlement. They settled at Parramatta, some ten miles from Sydney, ›ioneers of the active life among religious in Australia.

Near at hand was the prison which contained a great number of nmates, divided into three classes, according to the type of offence ommitted. Belonging to the first class were those women whose onduct was reasonably satisfactory and who soon would be ssigned, as domestics, to the various families in the colony. The econd class prisoners were mothers of illegitimate children; unfor-unate little ones who knew no other home than the prison cell. The women of the third class were poor degraded creatures, the ffscouring of human society, who had to undergo severe punish-nent, and whose usual occupation was breaking stones and sawing vood.

Violent and abusive, they frequently rebelled against their hard ›t, and once, while together at their work, were in such a state of evolt that the magistrate had to send for a company of soldiers to y and subdue them. When the men entered the yard the women egan to attack them with stones! The captain, in perplexity, said › the magistrate: "What are we to do? We cannot fire upon vomen or charge them with the bayonet!"

"Drive them back with their own weapons," was the reply. So ıe soldiers, whose aim was more accurate, succeeded in forcing the nhappy women back into their quarters where they were put under ›ck and key.

It was on these poor souls, not one of whom was beyond the ınge of God's mercy, that the Sisters of Charity chiefly concen-'ated, since their need of sympathy and understanding was the reatest. About 500 were Catholics, the vast majority of them years and years away from the Sacraments, and apparently wholly giver over to crime. The nuns, with their unlimited human kindness succeeded in unlocking their sad hearts, and by God's grace bring ing a ray of light into the spiritual darkness which had hithert enshrouded them.

Five mornings and evenings a week they came to the prison t give instruction. Each Sister sat on a chair in the yard surrounde by her own group of convicts. These squatted on the ground, fo the luxury even of benches was denied them. From the start th convicts, so lawless and contemptuous of authority, evinced th utmost respect and reverence for the nuns, and before two month were over the change effected in the women was remarkable. A ribaldry and obscene conversation ceased while oaths and curse were seldom heard. Most important of all, a general desire to fre quent the Sacraments became apparent, and the priest, who som time previously dared not approach certain sections of the place, s vile was the conduct of the women, with their screams and mockin cat-calls, now had to be helped by one or more of his fellow clerg to get through the number of confessions.

The Sisters, however, were not yet satisfied, and after much praye and deliberation the Superior, Mother Mary John, wrote to th Governor of the colony, Sir George Gipps, requesting an interview This was courteously granted, and on the day appointed she an Sister Mary Baptist presented themselves at Government House.

Reports of the improvements effected in the behaviour of th female convicts had reached headquarters, and not only was Hi Excellency most anxious to meet the " good ladies," but he was als desirous of doing anything in his power to help them in their work The nuns, unaware of his kind dispositions towards them, wer painfully nervous when ushered into his presence. Though h greeted them affably, motioned them to be seated on comfortabl chairs, and himself began the conversation with the usual prelim inary remarks on the weather, the salubrious quality of the climat and so forth, designed to set people at their ease, his well-mean efforts met with no great success. The Sisters felt too keenly th insecurity of their own position, for if they incurred the displeasur of the Government they might as well disappear altogether fror New South Wales.

After a few minutes he came straight to the point by saying: ' Now tell me in what way I can be of service to you?"

Mother Mary John drew in a deep breath. Her fingers clenched ınd unclenched beneath her cloak; so much depended on the answer he would receive. She flashed a glance at Sister Mary Baptist, ' Pray, pray," was what her eyes said.

" Your Excellency," she began diffidently, " as you know we have ıow spent some weeks in attendance at the convict prison."

Sir George nodded and felt he could guess what was coming next –a request for monetary aid.

" They'll get it, too," he thought. " They deserve to be supported n the fine work they are doing."

Aloud he said: " Daily I am hearing accounts of the good you re accomplishing, and I quite understand that you must be in need f support. If you will permit me, in the name of the British Govrnment, to offer you——"

A quick gesture from Mother Mary John caused him suddenly ɔ stop. " Oh, Sir!" she cried, " you misunderstand me; our own ;hurch will see to our upkeep. It is not for ourselves but for the oor women whom we visit that we ask help. It is a suggestion ıat we wish to make to you, that might raise the moral tone of ıe whole prison."

Sir George gazed at her in dumbfounded amazement. So it was ot money after all but an attempt to improve the prison regulaons; an attempt by ladies not two months in the colony, and Irish dies at that! Fortunately he was blessed with a keen sense of umour, and so with considerable amusement he asked them to nfold their plan. The laughter died out of his face, however, as Iother Mary John expounded their ideas.

" Your Excellency," she said, " by God's grace our work among ıe convicts has been blessed with a certain amount of success, but anything of lasting value to their souls is to be accomplished, there something that calls for alteration in the prison system, as it is ɔw in force."

" And that is?" he asked quietly, more impressed than he would ave cared to admit by the authority with which she spoke and

the simple dignity of her bearing. In her words and manner the
was now not a trace of nervousness.

"It is the work in which they are employed. Sawing wood an
breaking stones are occupations that are anything but upliftin
They tend, rather, to harden and degrade, partly on account of th
resentment which the women feel with regard to this form
labour. They have to be forced to do it at all, and kept to it b
constant threat of punishment. If other work could be substitute
work that would appeal to their instincts as women, we feel su
that the prison as a whole would be more easily managed." Sh
paused and shot a glance at Sir George to see how he was takin
it. Whether he was pleased or not he gave no sign but meditative
rubbed his chin and murmured: "Please continue. What do yo
suggest?"

"That the women be employed in laundry work. Not only wou
it be useful but it would encourage them in habits of cleanlines
Needlework could also be done. Embroidery, knitting, crochet,
these tend to have a calming and refining influence; they wou
give the women a new interest in life. Probably a number of the
are clever with their fingers already, and these could teach th
others. That's all, Your Excellency," she ended. "I hope you do
think we have made too bold in putting——"

"Not at all, not at all." Her half-uttered apology was brush
aside. "I think the plan might prove quite feasible. It's worth tr
ing, anyway." And the Sisters saw to their joy that his thin fa
was creased in smiles. "Of course you understand, though, that
must consult my subordinate officers; those directly in charge of t
women must agree to your suggestion before it can be put in
execution. If at all possible it shall be given a fair trial. I promi
you that much. Now," rising from his chair, "if you will pard
me a moment, I'll fetch my wife. I know she would like to me
you."

When they were alone Sister Mary Baptist heaved a big sigh
relief. Mother Mary John laughed softly. "We must pray much
thanksgiving," she said. "I never dreamt he would be so approa
able; much less that he would see our point so quickly. We mu
write this very evening to tell Mother Aikenhead about it all. Ca

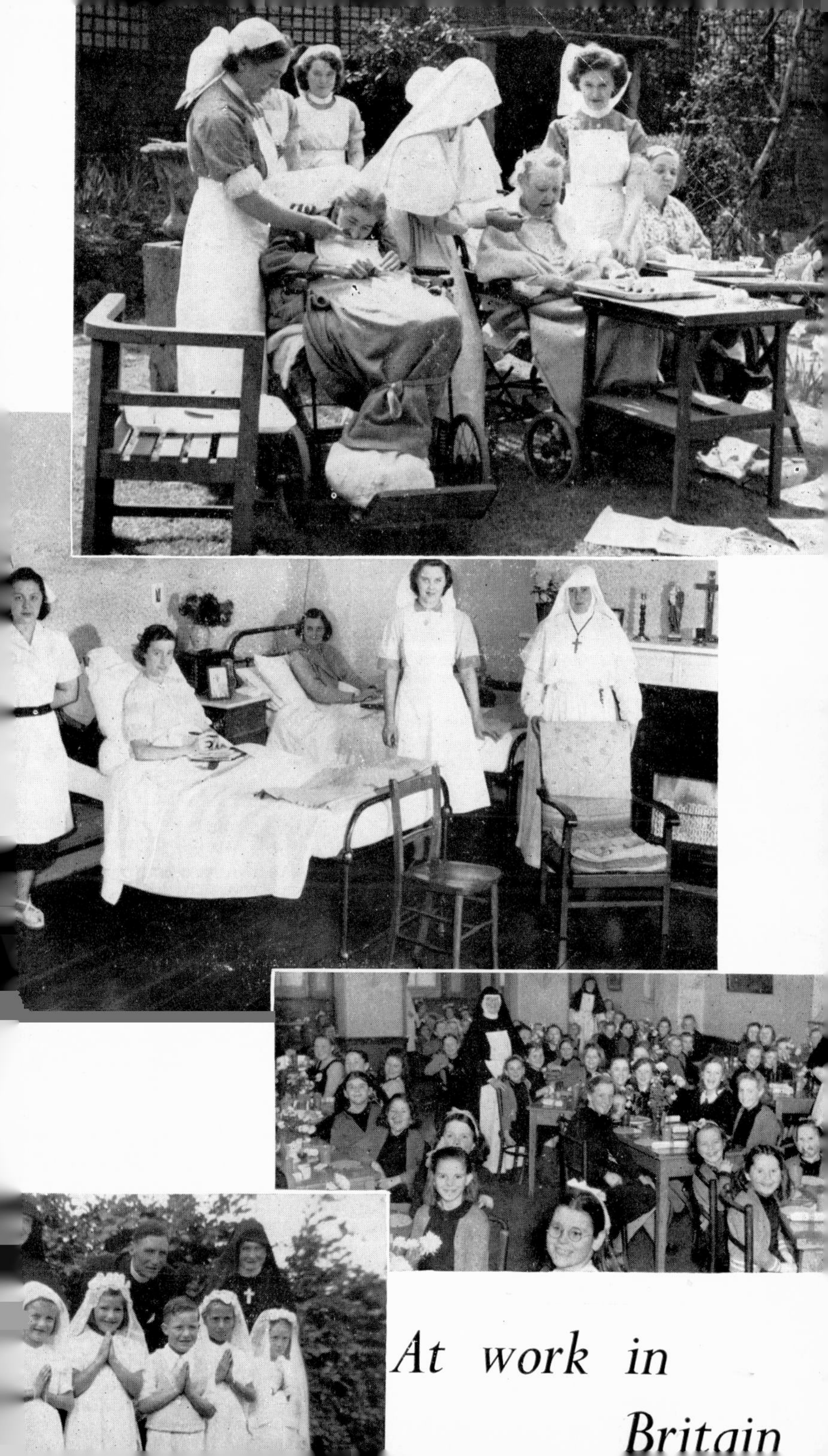

At work in Britain

Social Work

ɔu imagine the interest she'd take in our story, and all the 'Hail [arys' she'd say?"

"If only she could see us now, sitting in state . . ." but Sister [ary Baptist's remark remained unfinished, for at that instant Sir ·eorge and Lady Gipps entered the room. The latter was charm- ıg, and the visit ended pleasantly, though there was an awkward ıoment when wine and biscuits were produced. To such treatment ıe Sisters were utterly unaccustomed!

From that time on, the Governor and his wife were on excellent :rms with the nuns, whom they occasionally visited at their little ɔnvent and to whom they sent frequent gifts of fruit and vege- ıbles. Sir George saw to it that the suggestion of the Sisters was ırried out, and in a remarkably short time the prison was reformed. 'he magistrate and matron were so satisfied with the conduct of ıe women that not only were they assigned to private families as :rvants but they were allowed to receive wages. Thus they gradu- lly became independent of the Government and their self-respect 'as restored.

Enjoying thus the approval of the highest authority in the colony, ıe Sisters could work unhindered, save for outbursts of jealousy nd bitterness which their success occasioned in some circles. In ddition to their daily attendance at the prison, they visited the ick in the hospital and in their homes and gave religious instruc- ion in several schools. Later some of the small community moved ɔ Sydney where they took charge of orphan children. This proved ɔ be a task of heavy responsibility, as the little ones, some eighty n number, were lacking in every sort of moral training. Some vere so addicted to stealing that they would rise from their beds ıt night and search the pockets of their companions for the ' treasures " that appeal to youthful eyes. They would be found ɔrowling round the house, too, in search of food, not because they vere hungry but because they knew no better. Infinite patience, tact ınd gentleness were needed to win these little hearts for Christ. With His grace and His love the nuns succeeded.

Of all places, that dearest to the Sisters was the condemned cell, vhere their visit always brought hope and comfort and sometimes :ven joy. The gratitude shown by the men for the smallest act of kindness was very touching. One day they were warned not to approach a certain criminal who was branded as dangerous. The Sisters pleaded so earnestly to be allowed visit him that the warder reluctantly consented. "Little better than a wild beast," he grunted, unlocking the heavy door. Glaring at them from a corner where he crouched was the unhappy man. With his tangled hair and beard, his staring bloodshot eyes, he appeared ferocious enough to justify the warder's callous statement.

"What do you want?" he muttered.

"We've come to see you," replied Sister Francis de Sales.

"Well, you've seen me now, and a fine sight I make," was the ungracious response.

"You're speaking to ladies, so keep a civil tongue in your head," growled the warder, advancing as though to strike him. "None of your insolence you——"

"Stop!" cried Sister Francis de Sales, interposing herself between them. "Please will you wait outside. We wish to see this man alone," she said, in such a decided tone that the astonished warder found himself walking in the yard without quite knowing how he got there!

"You needn't be afraid," said the prisoner; and the Sisters noticed with surprise that the roughness was gone from his voice. "I am not a wild beast," he went on, "but they would make me one. There was nothing for me but irons and the lash," he shuddered, "never a Christian word. 'Twould break the spirit of any man."

The nuns nodded in sympathy. "Perhaps we could be of use to you now," said Sister Mary Laurence. "We're Irish Sisters of Charity and we——"

"You're Irish!" he cried incredulously, and forgetting the chains around his ankles, he tried to rise and go towards them. "So am I! Mickey Donohue from Clonakilty—at your service," he added whimsically.

"County Cork," smiled the nun. "We've come from Dublin; were you ever there?"

"Aye, many a time. It's a grand city, but you can't beat Cork! That's the place for me!" and the warder, standing outside with his ear to the door heard something resembling a chuckle coming from his "wild beast" of a prisoner, who two days later would face death like a hero.

In such a humble way did the pioneer nuns in Australia begin heir work for the poor of Christ, the poorest of the poor, the out-ast and the social leper. The difficulties of this type of mission can nly be guessed, but if their labours were hard, their lives lonely, heir poverty extreme, their consolations were many and God's lessing was lavished on their efforts. The ever-increasing spiritual arvest being reaped to-day by the daughters of Mary Aikenhead as reached proportions undreamt of by those five gallant women vho bravely ploughed the untilled earth and sowed the first seeds.

CHAPTER XVI

The Branching Tree

When one is only six years of age a silver shilling, especially if it be one's very first, is wealth untold, and little Christian Quan, her precious coin neatly wrapped in tissue paper and snugly tucked away in the corner of her purse, had already spent the best part of a week planning how she could make the most use of it. The shilling had opened up for her new horizons; it suggested boundless possibilities; it was nothing less than the key to Wonderland. When the poor beggar man came asking for help she could not bear to part with it but gave him instead her halfpenny. To be sure it was a very special kind of halfpenny for once (before she got the shilling) it, too, had been a treasure and still looked new and bright, rather like a sovereign, but for all that it was just a halfpenny.

"Thank you, missy," said the old man humbly, smiling at he gratefully; but he made no move to go and stood there looking a her with hungry pleading in his glance. Christian smiled too, bu when their eyes met she began to feel horribly uncomfortable. Onl too well, she feared, did he know that she had the shilling an didn't want to lose it. Her cheeks grew crimson as only a littl girl's can when she knows that she is acting meanly. Still she hesi tated; still he lingered. Then, as he turned to go, an awful though struck her: "Suppose he is really Our Lord in disguise, like th story Mammy told me!" Him she couldn't refuse, so the shilling tissue paper and all, found its way into the beggar's grimy hand while Christian tasted for the first time in her young life the un selfish joy of sacrifice.

It was a joy she was to taste many times thereafter, for she wa one of those chosen souls whom God leads by hard paths. As sh grew older she grew to love the poor ever more intensely and so i was no surprise when, at the age of twenty-two, she entered Mothe

Aikenhead's Congregation. Here she was blissfully happy. Yet though her whole life was henceforth to be devoted to the poor it was not to be spent as a Sister of Charity. After she had been some months in Stanhope Street she was asked once again by God to make a new sacrifice. Her mother fell ill and otherwise, too, family circumstances clearly showed that her duty lay at home. She returned then to her native city of Waterford. The remainder of her life was spent in hidden, humble service of those around her, chiefly her dearly loved friends the poor. Daily she prayed that the Sisters of Charity might come to Waterford where the need for them was so crying, where such a harvest of souls could be reaped. In due course her life of prayer and sacrifice bore fruit. In 1841 the Bishop asked Mother Aikenhead to establish a convent in the city on the Suir. Two Sisters were sent to prepare the way for the regular community, but as their house in Lady Lane was not yet ready they were offered hospitality by Christian Quan for a whole month.

Thus was founded the Convent of Our Lady of Charity in Waterford. It had many generous benefactors among the citizens, chief of whom was the Mayor himself, Mr. Meagher, father of Thomas Francis Meagher of "Young Ireland" fame. But perhaps the first stone of that successful house was laid thirty-eight years before when a very small girl made a very big sacrifice for one whom she took to be Our Lord in disguise. Nor was her mistake so great. "What you do unto the least of these my little ones you do unto Me."

* * * * * *

For the tenth time that morning, September 26th, 1848, Mother Mary Agnes unfolded Mother Aikenhead's letter and read it slowly through. She gazed on the words as if dumbfounded, unable to grasp their full meaning, but returning always to one sentence that stood out in words of fire: "I am most truly grieved that the unwilling measure of withdrawing the little community has become necessary. . . ."

For eight years the Sisters of Charity had been working in Preston, where their schools were almost twice the size of those in Ireland. A night school for the factory workers and a very large mission to the sick offered great scope for apostolic zeal. Unfortunately, however, the needed help was not forthcoming. Owing to a misunderstanding between the priests in charge of the parish and the nuns there were no funds to support the convent. Thus the first English foundation seemed doomed to come to a speedy and calamitous end. The Sisters toiled on year after year in straitened circumstances amidst many difficulties, till at last it seemed clear to Mother Aikenhead that in justice to the Congregation she could no longer allow this state of affairs to continue. It was one of those unfortunate situations encountered so often in the history of religious orders; advance is impossible and the only escape seems to lie in retreat.

Mother Aikenhead's decision brought real sorrow to the community, for they had been hoping against hope that some way out of the difficulty would be found. It looked now as if that was not to be, so they quietly set about making preparations for departure. All around, the poor people were storming heaven with prayers that their friends might not be taken from them.

A month passed and the Sisters of Charity were on board the packet boat for Ireland. As the Welsh mountains disappeared behind them in the haze the chapter was closed and the joys and sorrows of their years at Preston swallowed up in the mists of eternity.

* * * * * *

Galway Bay! We think of the song—played, hummed, whistled, crooned, even parodied—transmitting to that charming area in our western coast something of the glamour of Hollywood. Very different were the associations a hundred years ago, when at Clarinbridge, not far from the great Atlantic, the Sisters of Charity took possession of their new convent, Our Lady's Priory. Their coming to the West was due entirely to the generosity of a lady named Mrs. Redington, who, distressed by the poverty and ignorance of the local people, had begged Mother Aikenhead to send them a community. She promised to give the foundation every help in her power. This she certainly did, for not only did she give them a convent, able to support five sisters, but she gave them also a chapel, beautifully equipped, and twelve acres of land. She spared neither trouble nor expense. Her delicate kindness did much to counterbalance the grief of Mother Aikenhead, who shared as fully in the joys of her daughters at Clarinbridge as she did in the trials of those at Preston, looking on the good fortune and the bad as equally God's will.

One great obstacle which the Sisters had to contend with was the havoc wrought amongst the people by the proselytisers. Taking advantage of the prevailing penury these had induced many unfortunate little ones to exchange their spiritual birthright for a mess of pottage. Many a year was to pass before the effects of their baneful efforts were completely wiped out. One of the first tasks, therefore, that the nuns had to undertake was the opening of a school. Their accommodation was limited so they had to reject many who applied for admission. A number of the grown girls and young women had not yet received the Sacraments and these were given preference over the rest. The mothers of the neighbourhood, not knowing the reason for the Sisters' choice, jumped to the conclusion that the older the child was the better the chance of her being accepted as a student, so Peggy, Noreen or Bridgie-Anne surprised themselves as well as the nuns by passing from eight, nine, eleven, to ten, eleven, thirteen years in the space of twenty-four hours. With learning as the prize the West was feverishly wide awake!

* * * * * *

"I'll never love anybody again," Letitia told herself fiercely; "never, never, never," she choked, as the first spadeful rattled down on the oak coffin. Thick and fast the clay fell then and beneath it lay the last human being to whom Letitia would give her heart in this world. When all was over, guided by a little group of friends and sympathisers, she walked from the churchyard with unseeing eyes.

Letitia was barely out of her 'teens but death had already played a large part in her life. One of the earliest and saddest recollections of her childhood was of herself sobbing in a dark room and crying "Dadda! Dadda!" to someone who lay stiff and cold on a bed, his ears closed for ever to her voice. Eight years later God had taken her mother also. Sam remained, and their love for one another had brought them through many a lonely hour. Now he, too, was gone, and there was nothing left to her but an empty house and the memory of a frail young boy who had smiled bravely to the end.

"Letty, Letty, can't you give a fellow a chance?" he used to cry in playful protest whenever she insisted rather too firmly on the doctor's orders being carried out to the letter. "Letty, Letty——" she could hear him still.

Letitia Bradshaw's father had been a wealthy man with considerable property in Tipperary. From a worldly point of view she was very well off. Nor was money her only heritage. From her father there had come, too, a far more important spiritual legacy, the Catholic Faith. After his death their mother, a strict Protestant, had brought the children up in her own religion. When she, in her turn died, the child Letitia, now aged twelve, took Sam's hand in hers and went with him to the parish priest.

"Please, Father, will you make us Catholics," she demanded. Amused by what he thought to be a childish fancy he put them off for the moment, but when he found that their fervour did not diminish and that they were determined to grow up Catholics he instructed them and received them into the Church.

From that day forward they had been exemplary in the practice of their religion and so it was natural that Letitia, when left without a near relative in the world, should turn to God for consolation. Though she gradually came to accept generously the cross that was laid on her young shoulders, she could not help asking herself why all this should have happened to her—why she should have been chosen for deep sorrow; why the human pleasure of a home should be denied to her. Why? Why? Why? It was a long, long time before the answer came.

Years passed before the day dawned when Letitia realised that her heart was no longer her own. She was in love. All she had she would give to Him, who would be hers for eternity. Never more would she wonder why God had taken those dearest to her. The answer was obvious: He wanted her more completely for Himself. Gladly, then, she responded to the call: "Go, sell what thou hast and give to the poor and come, follow Me." She obeyed the injunction literally. In disposing of her "great possessions" amongst the poor she set aside a sum for the founding of a convent in her native county. There would be yet another earthly home for the Son of Man Who had once complained that He had not whereon to lay His head.

"Our Lady of the Angels," Clonmel, was opened in 1845. The accounts which frequently reached Mother Aikenhead of the good work being done in Tipperary brought joy unspeakable to her spirit. Sister Mary Emilian Bradshaw, on her part, thanked God that there were Sisters of Charity visiting the sick, relieving the destitute and instructing the ignorant, in a place where no such blessing would have been enjoyed had not she herself received a religious vocation. Her work meanwhile was in the wards of St. Vincent's Hospital, where she laboured unceasingly to serve the sick and afflicted.

* * * * * *

". . . and so," continued the youthful story-teller, "this old ruin was once a monastery and real monks lived here long ago."

"How long?" demanded Georgina, who was literal-minded.

"I wouldn't be too sure," replied Daniel vaguely; "anyway, hundreds and hundreds of years. I must ask Papa; he would know exactly when the monks first came to Benada."

"What a pity they aren't here now," murmured Mary dreamily. She gazed at the high, ivy-covered tower with its crumbling moss-grown steps. "Can't you just imagine them walking up and down under these shady trees joining their voices with the birds in singing the praises of God!"

A chuckle came from James and he said in a patronising tone: "Our Mary is getting romantic."

"Indeed, no," his sister denied, "it's only that I never knew before that this was a *real* abbey with monks and an abbot and a chapel——"

"And a refectory and cells and a chapter house and all that you read about in books," added Daniel. "Our family didn't come to Sligo till sixteen hundred and—and—something. I forget what, nine or ten, perhaps, when Sir Roger Jones, who lived in Wales, took the abbey from the monks because the King told him he could have it."

"But how could the King give it to him when he didn't own it?" Georgina objected.

"They did things like that in those days," answered Daniel;

"that's how all the Irish people lost their property. When Sir Roger got Benada he drove away the monks and built the house we live in. Then the abbey gradually decayed; no one cared about it any more. Sir Roger was a Protestant, you see, and didn't like monks. Years and years afterwards another Jones became a Catholic—he was our great, great grand-uncle Roger whose picture hangs on the drawing-room wall. And that's how we're Catholics too."

"Poor old monks," sighed Georgina sadly. She patted the rough stone wall. "How they must have hated leaving this lovely place."

"Yes," nodded Mary, "and isn't it strange to think that our home, Benada Abbey, isn't really ours at all." Her voice dropped as she almost whispered: "This is holy ground and belongs to—God. Perhaps some day He may take it back again."

A deep silence fell upon the four "children of the Abbey," as they were known locally, a silence broken only by the rush of the River Moy flowing along by the little glade where they sat—Mary and Daniel on their favourite seat, a fallen tree trunk, James lying at full length in the luxurious grass at their feet. Georgina, a short distance away, made a charming picture in her green dress with her red-gold curls tumbling about her shoulders. Her back leaned against the dark grey tower; her chubby face was upturned to watch the patches of blue sky come and go as the soft wind gently stirred the canopy of leaves overhead.

After a few moments James spoke. "I'm tired of thinking," he declared. "Can't somebody say something, or let's play a game. I know," jumping up suddenly, "let's be monks and go round in our bare feet singing hymns."

"And fasting and sleeping on the hard ground," went on Daniel, with a knowing look at Mary. "Monks eat nothing but fish and berries."

James pondered a while. "Then I'd rather be Sir Roger," he decided, "coming to drive you out of the abbey," and he emitted a blood-curdling yell that made Georgina clap her hands with joy and shout at the top of her little lungs, "Oh, yes, yes, we'll all be monks!"

"You and Mary won't," said James rounding on her. "Who ever heard of lady monks? You go and play with your dolls."

"Oh, Daniel, please let us," and her eyes threatened tears as she appealed to the elder boy.

Daniel shook his head. "James is right, I'm afraid. Girls can't be monks, but they can be nuns. Wouldn't that be just as good?"

"'Twouldn't, I want to be a monk," she wailed. "You're mean, mean things an' I hate you."

"There, there, darling," soothed Mary, gently placing her arm about the little one's shoulders. "You and I'll be nuns together. Suppose we let the boys play here and we'll have our own convent at the other side of the chapel. You can be the Reverend Mother, too; that'll be nice, won't it?"

Georgina brightened. "Maybe," she admitted grudgingly, as she allowed herself to be led gently from the "abbey," where already "Brother Daniel" was on his knees rapt in contemplation, unaware of the wicked "Sir Roger Jones," who, armed to the teeth, lurked behind the bushes waiting to pounce upon his victim.

Perhaps it was due to the fact that they were, as Mary put it, "brought up on holy ground"; perhaps it was the prayers of the ancient monks; whatever it was, the children of the abbey, as they grew up, heard one by one the call of God. Daniel and Mary were the first to break the family circle—he to join the Society of Jesus, she to join the Sisters of Charity. Later on James and Georgina followed in their steps. A third girl became a Sister of Mercy. When Freddy, the youngest boy, died there was no one of the family left but the widowed mother, a fragile, queenly lady who had grown old as gracefully as a silver birch. She begged Mother Aikenhead to found a convent at Benada; and that is how, after two centuries and a half, the Lord of Glory returned to the Tabernacle within which He had so long dwelt.

In July, 1858, three Sisters of Charity came, in the name of the Congregation, to accept the gift of Benada. Two of these were Mary, now Sister Mary Attracta, and Georgina, now Mother Mary Justinian, for the "Reverend Mother" of their childish play was a Reverend Mother now in reality.

That night the sky for miles around was red with light reflected from the bonfires kindled at the crossroads. Such was the royal welcome given to the nuns by the people of the district. Meanwhile in the ruined chapel the ghostly chant of the Te Deum Laudamus mingled with the hooting of a solitary owl.

* * * * * *

And so, like a tree, Mother Aikenhead's Congregation put forth its first branches. Many others were to follow, lifting one by one their " leafy arms to pray," stretching outwards and upwards in the sunshine of God's love.

The High Altar, Our Lady's Hospice, Harolds Cross, Dublin.

CHAPTER XVII

A Pair of Brown Eyes

ELLEN WRIGHT, alone in the girl's dormitory at Stanhope Street, was feeling particularly sorry for herself one hot afternoon at the end of August in the year 1821. A sick headache is unpleasant at the best of times but when it chooses to come on the Rev. Mother's Feast Day—well, that really is the last straw, especially when through the open window floats the sound of one's companions thoroughly enjoying the extra recreation granted in honour of the day.

"Just my luck to miss all the fun," she thought. "Oh dear, how I——"

"Ellen," came a soft whisper from the door, "are you awake?"

"Yes," said Ellen fretfully, "and I wish I wasn't. I haven't slep' a wink all day and it's dead lonely up here."

"You poor thing," said Mary sympathetically, going over to the bed. "I guessed you'd feel bad at missin' all the fun so I coaxed Sister Jerome to let me up for five minutes. The others send you their love and hope you're feelin' better."

"I can't say that I am," came the doleful response, "but I'm real glad to see you, Mary; you're the kindest girl to think of me. Have you had a grand day?"

Mary nodded and seated herself at the foot of the bed. "'Twas a shame you weren't down for the dinner—Irish stew an' custard an'——"

"Irish stew, custard——" groaned Ellen, turning green. "Don't mention such things," and she shuddered realistically.

"Oh lor! I'm sorry!" cried Mary contritely. "There, now, I've gone and upset you. I won't talk about anything like that any more. Ellen"—she lowered her voice to a whisper—"I have something to tell you though, something that happened yesterday after Sister'd sent you to bed. Cross your heart you won't tell a soul."

"Yes?" Ellen's curiosity was aroused and she eyed her friend expectantly, "do go on."

"Well, it was like this," began Mary, smacking her lips with relish. "It was nearly five o'clock and we were finishin' off in the ironin' room when in came Rev. Mother, Sister Jerome and a crowd of visitors. There was an old lady, three young ones, a little girl and—and a gentleman. Sister gave us a look as much as to say 'Keep your eyes down and get on with your work,' so we all started bein' awful busy but I tell you we kept our ears well open."

Ellen smiled faintly. "And what did you hear?"

"'Twas very little then, but after a bit they went around the room an' when they came to my table they stopped an' one of the young ladies asked me about the lace collar I was ironin'. Then they passed on but I heard one of them say: 'What a lovely brunette!' 'Twas such a funny word I kep' starin' after them kind of puzzled. Then—then the man looked round and smiled real nice at me, and Ellen, do you know it made me feel all queer—sort of happy like. He pulled one of the ladies back and sez he to her: 'Did you ever see such eyes? She's a stunner and no mistake.' Along came Sister Jerome an' asked him what he was lookin' at an' he told her he was only admirin' the lovely room. Queer, isn't it, the way them grand people talk. Did you ever hear of a brunette or a stunner?"

"Well, I suppose a stunner would be somethin' that would stun a body, but I never heard tell of a brunette. Would you ask Sister Jerome?"

"You needn't fear; it might be some class of a sin, and yet it couldn't be for she said *I* was it—'a lovely brunette!'"

"There's a dictionary in the schoolroom," suggested Ellen, "why not try if the word is in it."

"Indeed and I will, though I'm not sure how to spell it, but do you know what I think it means?" Ellen shook her head.

"That I'm good-lookin'! Now tell me, am I?" and with a quick gesture she pulled off her cap, shook loose her dark curly hair and with wide-eyed eagerness awaited the verdict.

"Workin' girls like us have no call to be good-lookin'," came the blunt reply. "A pretty face never yet ironed a shirt, but I suppose you're passable." The note of jealousy in her voice went unheeded by Mary, who, suddenly realising she had been considerbly longer than five minutes, announced: "I'd better be goin'. There'll be just time before Benediction——"

"Time for what?" queried Ellen.

"To find out what a brunette is," and she whisked out of the oom.

There was no doubt about it but Mary Gibbons was a beautiful girl. Tall and slender, she carried herself with a grace that even he clumsy institution clothes could not disguise, while her dark rown velvety eyes, deep pools of innocence, reflected the candour of her soul. Thanks to her sweet temper, her kindly heart and eadiness to oblige, she was a general favourite, and the fact that she had been hitherto unconscious of both her looks and her popularity made her all the more charming. But from the day she realised she was attractive a sad change came over her. It was Ellen who noticed it first when, on going into the dormitory one morning, she found Mary standing on a bed peering at her reflection in a large picture of the "Flight into Egypt" that hung on the wall. Mirrors were considered a luxury, not a necessity, in the Stanhope Street of those years and she had, therefore, to use her ingenuity if she wished to see her pretty face. Gradually she became restless and unsettled; repeatedly then she begged Sister Jerome to find her a situation outside, for, as she confessed frankly to Ellen, "I'm tired of livin' with nuns and women."

The Sister was rather surprised at first, for Mary had always appeared happy and contented, but as most of the girls, on coming o eighteen or nineteen years of age, had positions found for them, she promised to speak to Mother Aikenhead on the subject. To place a girl like Mary offered no difficulty, for she had a good character and was a splendid worker, so one of Mrs. O'Brien's riends was only too delighted to take her as a housemaid.

It was a raw November afternoon when Mary Gibbons, with her worldly possessions in a little tin trunk, bade farewell to Stanhope Street.

"You'll come back and see us often, won't you, Mary?" asked Mother Aikenhead as the cab which was to take ner to her new home pulled up at the door. "There'll always be a welcome for ou here."

"Thank you, Rev. Mother," replied the girl, "and thank you

for all you and Sister Jerome have done for me. Will you pray for me, please, Rev. Mother?" she added.

"Certainly, dear child, of course I shall remember you. God be with you now and always. Don't forget a little prayer for us."

From the cab window Mary smiled and for the last time Mother Aikenhead saw the beautiful brown eyes.

Where Mary Gibbons had come from nobody knew. She had been already in the House of Refuge some years before the Sisters of Charity had taken it over. She herself had but the faintest recollection of her early life. Her mother she dimly remembered but of her father she had never known anything; nor had she ever wondered why his name was never mentioned.

Her first situation lasted exactly a month. By that time the eldest son had not only fallen violently in love with her but had declared his intention of marrying her at once. Mary was given the choice of returning to Stanhope Street or going as a servant to two elderly ladies. She chose the latter, for though little to her liking, she would at least have her freedom. One morning the ladies came downstairs to find no breakfast ready. Mary was gone! Scrupulously honest, she had taken nothing with her but her own belongings. Her descent was very rapid after that. Like a daughter of Eve she grasped at forbidden fruit. Before six months had passed she might have been seen at night loitering around the quays or strolling up and down Capel Street as another Mary Gibbons had done long before, her manner bold, her eyes inviting—a Magdalen of the great city.

For ten years this was her life. Mother Aikenhead never failed to pray for her poor stray lamb, though all efforts to trace her proved fruitless. Yet on three or four occasions Sisters visiting Jervis Street Hospital passed by the end of her bed unaware that its Protestant occupant, Elizabeth Smith, was none other than Rev. Mother's "Mary" about whom they had so often been instructed to make enquiries.

* * * * * *

One evening in the year 1832 Mary Gibbons was returning to the house where she lodged, a disreputable den in an unsavoury neighbourhood. When about to enter the hall door some invisible

Help for the Dying

Under the Southern Cross

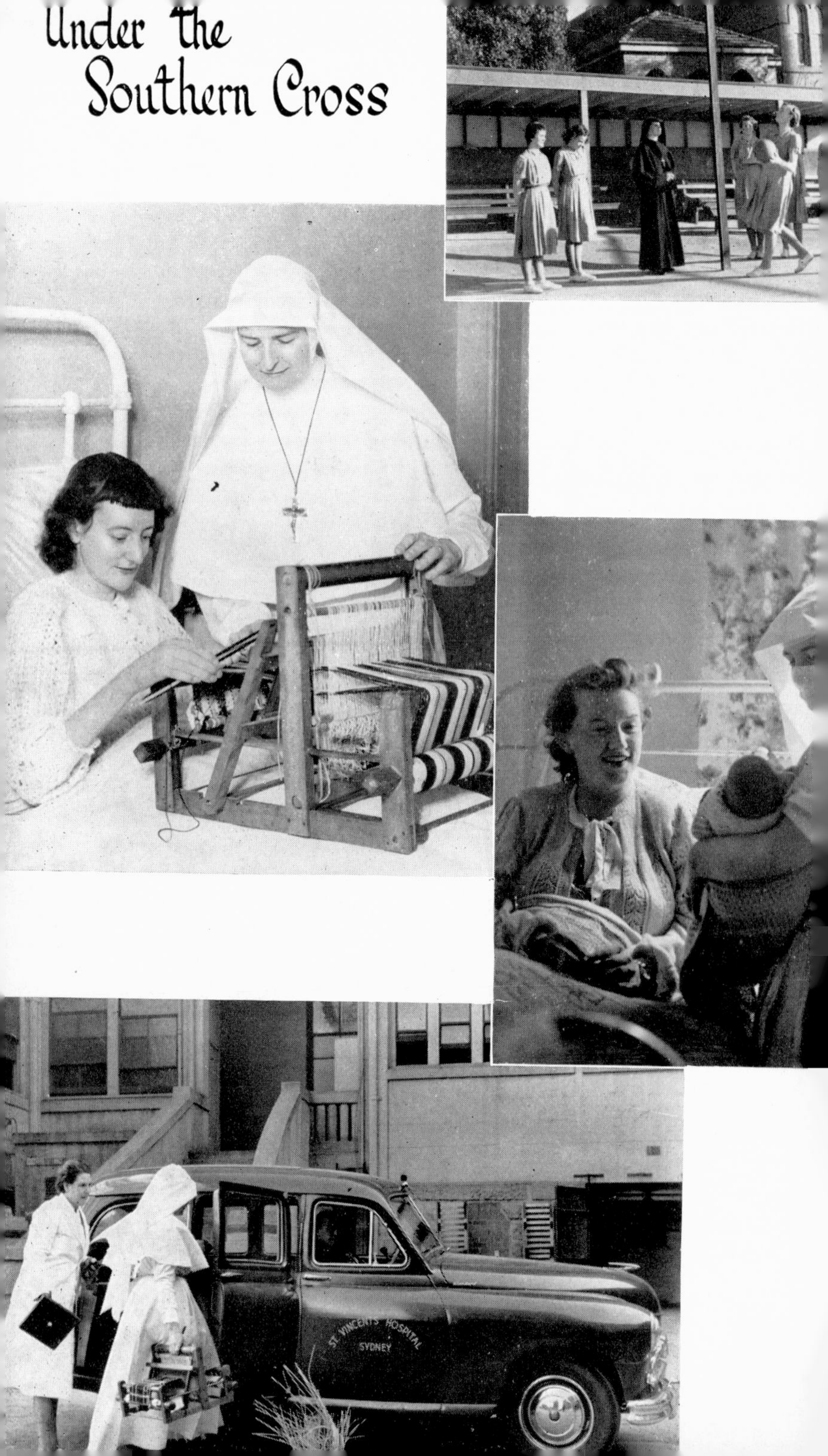

obstacle seemed to bar her way and keep her back. Again and again she tried to go in but the same mysterious force repelled her. Terrified she did the only thing possible: turned and ran swiftly away, neither knowing nor caring where she went.

"What's the hurry, Mary?" called a man's voice from a laneway as she sped past. But Mary gave no heed and left him staring open-mouthed after her.

At Marlboro' Street Church the clerk was about to lock the door when up the steps she ran and tried to force her way inside.

"I want a priest, I want a priest," she gasped, her breath coming in painful jerks and her temples throbbing.

"Is it a sick call?"

"No—no—I must go to Confession."

"Wisha, ma'am, you should 'a been here an hour ago. The priests were sittin' all the evenin'. Go home now like a good woman. You can be heard in the mornin'."

"But I haven't a home!" cried Mary in desperation, "and I can't go back *there*. Oh please, please help me," and she caught his arm imploringly.

Tom Kelly was a chivalrous man and beauty in distress called up the kindness that lay beneath his gruff exterior. "Take it aisy now, ma'am," he said soothingly. "If it's lodgings you want I know a woman that'd take you in. It's a *respectable* place, though."

The emphasis on the word did not escape her and for the first time for many a day the hot blushes surged over her cheeks and she knew what it was to feel shame. Tom locked the door, slipped the great key into his pocket and moved away from the church with Mary following meekly in his wake. All her bravado, all her bold insolence, had fallen from her like a cloak, and few of her associates would have recognised in the trembling girl the handsome brunette whose dark eyes were so dangerously alluring.

Thanks to his kindly intervention a room was procured for her at no great distance from the church and there she was installed for the night, but not to sleep, for hardly had the stout landlady creaked her way down the protesting staircase than Mary became aware that she was not alone. It seemed to her that eyes stared at her from the depths of a dark corner—eyes set in a grinning white face, while a mocking voice called "Mary, Mary!"

Half-paralysed with fear she felt as though her knees were giving way, while an ice-cold perspiration covered her face and hands. "My God, my God," she whispered, "have mercy on me!"

"She calls on God," cried a jeering voice, followed by a snort of laughter. Suddenly, on the wall in front of her, there appeared a vision of hell—a blazing furnace whose scorching breath filled the little room with an intolerable odour. Her ears were deafened by the cries of the damned. Many of these she recognised as her former companions. . . . Fascinated she gazed and gazed; not a sound could she utter till the hungry flames shot out as though about to devour herself. When the fire touched her she screamed. A moment later the door was opened violently and in strode the man of the house. The room was empty save for Mary weeping hysterically in the corner.

"Get out of here," he shouted, as he seized her roughly by the shoulders. "I want no drunken women in this house."

"I'm not drunk," cried Mary. "Oh, for God's sake have pity on me!"

"She's sober, John, all right," panted his wife. "Maybe 'tis her mind is gone, the poor creature."

"Drunk or mad, she'll get out of here. Call the watchman, one of you," he shouted down to the little crowd of neighbours who had heard the screams and had come running to the house scenting trouble, or at least excitement.

Mary was arrested and locked in a tiny cell at the watch-house. There she fell on her knees and once more called on God to be merciful to her, for the terror of the vision still caused her limbs to tremble. In answer to her cry she seemed in her frenzy to hear a voice say: "Unless you take out your eyes you cannot be saved." Into her mind flashed Our Lord's own words: "If thy right eye scandalise thee, pluck it out. . . ." She did so. Then in her tortured mind she fancied she heard the words "Take out the other." She obeyed.

The condition in which they found her on the following morning must be left to the imagination. She was brought to Jervis Street Hospital and hovered for days between life and death. She recovered at last, remained in the hospital for almost a year, and then was welcomed back by Mother Aikenhead with open arms. It was the prodigal's wish to spend the rest of her life as a penitent with the Sisters of Charity.

* * * * * *

In Dublin of the early nineteenth century there were but three asylums for Magdalens. One in Lower Leeson Street was for Protestants. It was opened in 1767 by Lady Arbella Denny and was believed to be the first of its kind in Ireland. Another, in Dorset Street, was founded in 1794 for the "reception and employment of women leaving the Lock Hospital and desirous of returning into the paths of industry and virtue." The third, in Townsend Street, bore the name of the General Magdalen Asylum. This was founded in 1798 by a working man named Quarterman and a woman named Bridget Burke, who organised a penny collection to rent a house "for the reception of unfortunate females who, anxious to quit the paths of prostitution, prefer repentance and virtue to infamy and guilt." A Mrs. Ryan, niece to Archbishop Troy, was placed in charge and under her capable direction the women were able to support themselves respectably by laundry and needlework. In 1833, when age and ill-health prevented Mrs. Ryan from continuing her good work any longer, the Sisters of Charity took over the asylum from her.

The house was already greatly overcrowded, and this, together with the fact that it was in bad repair and unfavourably situated, determined Mother Aikenhead to look for suitable premises. The search was rewarded in 1837, when Donnybrook Castle was purchased. On the Feast of Our Lady of the Rosary of that year the penitents migrated from the noisy back street within the city to the pleasant mansion with its gardens and wooded fields. There was the added attraction that the place was within easy driving distance of St. Vincent's Hospital.

A winding country road bordered by thick hedges led from Leeson Street Bridge, beyond which the boundaries of the city barely extended, to the little village of Donnybrook, a street of straggling cottages, at the further end of which lay St. Mary Magdalen's Asylum.

There Mother Aikenhead occasionally stayed, for she looked on the house as a haven of rest and peace. Austerity was in the atmosphere, yet the Sisters were wonderfully happy, however monotonous and difficult their work. Not all the penitents were of the Mary Gibbons type, eager to atone for former sin. Many of them had come to the Home as to a prison, at the behest of parents or guardians who had found them wild, unmanageable, exposed by flightiness of character to the worst of evils. These girls, finding their captivity irksome, proceeded to "take it out" on the nuns by refusing to work, feigning illness and, in general, making life hard for those around them. There were others, more like Mary, who had come of their own free will to do penance, but who, when the "fierce joy of repentance" waned, found themselves pining once more for "fleshpots" and freedom. They insisted on leaving, only to fall into trouble again when settled in their familiar haunts.

No one understood better than Mother Aikenhead the many trials and difficulties with which those engaged in the Asylum had to contend. She once wrote: "The care of penitents brings much anxiety, and as far as I have had experience, is that station of our holy servitude which brings the least produce in the way of our desired recompense. We have less of the true comfort of observing desirable results than in any other of our holy functions. But if one mortal sin be prevented, well, ought we to rejoice. . . ."

This was a happiness they very often did experience, together with what St. Francis de Sales calls the greatest of all joys, that of winning a soul to God.

Eighteen years passed and Mary Gibbons, for long the most gentle, the most reserved, the most patient and industrious of penitents, lay dying. A Sister praying beside her marvelled at her holy dispositions. Here, indeed, was a soul inundated with divine grace. The Sister could not refrain from putting a question: "Tell me, Mary, had you in your younger days a great devotion to the Mother of God?"

The blind woman shook her head: "Not that I can think of, Sister."

"Can you think of nothing that you ever did that could have won for you such blessings?"

"I might have been in hell," said Mary simply, "for there was many a night when I stood lookin' down at the river an' wishin' to God I was under the water." She paused, and an expression of horror passed over her face as though she were living through it all once more. "Sister," she said slowly, "there's just one thing I can remember doin'—when I went to live in that—that bad house first, there was a picture of the Blessed Virgin. I took it off the wall and out of the house thinkin' it was no fittin' place for the Holy Mother of God. I dunno, but maybe she was pleased with that. I never did anything else but to hurt her Blessed Son—but I'm sorry, real, real sorry, an' I'll never . . ." her voice broke off as the Angelus bell rang, and before the prayer was ended the soul of the "lovely brunette" was winging its way to Heaven.

Nursing the Cholera Patients in Grangegorman.

CHAPTER XVIII

The Mother in the Home

A SISTER of Charity who knew Mother Aikenhead well paid her the following tribute:

"In my young days," she said, "I was much struck with the family spirit or spirit of union encouraged and propagated in all our houses, especially in the convent where Rev. Mother resided. All . . . felt themselves at home wherever she was . . . she was truly the large-hearted Mother."

When in 1845 a new foundation was made at Harold's Cross, an area that was then almost open country, Mother Aikenhead went there to live, and Our Lady's Mount, as the new house was called, succeeded St. Stephen's Green as the focal point of the Congregation.

Though she left "the dear hospital" with profound regret, she found herself wonderfully refreshed by the change. The sweet, clear air, the birds singing in the trees, the play of light and shade on the luxuriant green foliage or on the still surface of the pond, the dewy freshness of the grass under the early morning sun were pleasures all the more appreciated by one who for years had been virtually a prisoner in a little room at the top of St. Vincent's. Indeed, as old age advanced, her admiration for the beauties of nature seemed to increase rather than diminish, and she was often to be found gazing in rapt silence at the glory of the sunset, or gently caressing the soft petals of a delicate flower, while the tender expression in the deep-set grey eyes betokened to those around that her thoughts were fixed on God, the Fount and Origin of all loveliness.

In such a pleasant setting, far from the busy hum of city streets, the last years of her life would be spent in peace but certainly not in idleness. In 1845, she had been appointed Mother General for life, so that death alone could relieve her of the heavy burden of responsibility. The direction of ten convents, all engaged in important, varied and absorbing work, lay in her hands, for though each house had its own Superior, more often than not she was young or inexperienced and in sore need of guidance. Then, too, difficulties of one sort or another were always cropping up which Mother Aikenhead would be called upon to solve.

Her chief and, indeed, her only means of contact with all save the Dublin convents was by letter. After 1828 she never again visited Cork; the foundations at Preston, Waterford, Clarinbridge and Clonmel she had never seen; yet she frequently astonished her distant communities with her accurate knowledge of their interior arrangements and outward surroundings. They did not realise that she looked upon them all with a mother's eye and that no detail, however trivial, that was once told to her escaped her memory. Her " poor lame pen," as she playfully called it, was always at the service of her children. Sometimes she wrote lying down; at other times propped up, generally at the cost of much pain. Her right arm, practically powerless, had to be supported on a cushion and the quill placed between the helpless fingers. Thus the 1,500 letters which are still extant, and possibly many more, were laboriously and painfully written.

Full of variety and highly characteristic, their range is considerable: short gossipy notes giving items of interest to those far away, advice as to the choice of a cow or turkeys, " a little bit of cash " for the purchase of these, a recommendation that the Sisters on the mission be provided with umbrellas, then long, closely-written pages dealing with many aspects of religious life—charity, prayer, the vows, union with God, to mention but a few. In their very simplicity her letters are self-revealing. In one she writes:

" Do, dear child, try to love your Heavenly Spouse while you are young. The heart grows hard and chilly with age. . . ."

It was once said of her that she could pass without any apparent effort from the depths of a clothes basket to the heights of Heaven!

Feast days and anniversaries were always remembered, and on those occasions a gift accompanied the letter, money, perhaps, or a book or a picture or, a little " extra " for the refectory. If there were children in the house they would not be forgotten either, and many a time her health was drunk in lemonade, and cakes eaten in her honour. Her efforts to supply all these cost her no small trouble. Great was her satisfaction when she could put by a trifle from time to time in an old leather purse kept near her for these special purposes.

When the weather was fine her correspondence was done in the garden, under the shade of an ancient elm or a wide-branched sycamore. There she would sit for hours, her writing table before her, while Dandy, the faithful friend, his head resting on his paws, lay on the grass and gazed into her face with adoring eyes.

She was hardly ever left long without interruptions. Sisters from other houses called on business; priests who had undertaken works of charity sought help or advice; young ladies came to settle their vocations. The week-ends usually brought a visitor from St. Vincent's Hospital, sometimes Mother Francis Magdalen, sometimes Sister Mary Camillus, sometimes a Sister in need of a little fresh air. Mrs. O'Brien, too, came regularly, for she never lost her interest in the House of Refuge at Stanhope Street. A group of girls who worked in the factories near Harold's Cross might be seen around lunch time coming up the avenue for a few minutes' chat, certain that their tales would find a sympathetic hearing. One, perhaps, had the worry of a sick parent; another had a brother who was " wild "; a third found the course of true love running far from smoothly. For each there was a word of consolation.

On the rare occasions when the Rev. Mother was left in comparative leisure, undisturbed by callers, Dandy, bored by the empty silence, would thrust his nose up under her elbow and gently lick her left hand to remind her that he, at least, was there and would welcome a few wise words or a scratch behind the ears.

Our Lady's Mount was an old-fashioned country residence with comfortable accommodation for twelve people. Once Mother Aikenhead made it her home it became the Mother House of the Congregation. To join the community of professed Sisters there came then Mother Mary Lucy and twenty novices. It was quite an exercise in artful manœuvring to fit everybody in. Quarters were very cramped at first, but after some time a new building (which comprised a chapel, a refectory and a number of cells), relieved the congestion.

Night classes were conducted for the factory girls; a Sunday School was organised and, of course, the sick poor in the extensive and impoverished district round Francis Street were visited daily. After a few years a large school was built within the convent grounds and near enough for the sound of tables and spellings, chanted by childish trebles, to be wafted to Rev. Mother's ears as she sat outside under a spreading tree or inside at the window of her room.

Long years of suffering had taken their inevitable toll. In addition to the spinal trouble which rendered her right arm almost useless and forced her to lie prostrate for hours each day, Mother Aikenhead was afflicted by rheumatism, bronchitis and severe headaches. About her mouth and beneath her eyes lines of pain were etched; while her poor back was made tender all over by the applications of leeches, blisters or scarificators. The remedies of those days often caused as much discomfort as the disease; and there were no modern drugs and no pain-killing needles.

Except in her letters, wherein she apologised occasionally for delay in replying, caused by illness, she scarcely ever referred to her own state of health. She was far more concerned with those of her children who were sick. Her sympathy was lavished on these, more especially on a novice or a postulant should one happen to fall ill, since she understood perfectly the fear of being sent home that strikes terror into the hearts of those not yet admitted to vows.

Once there was a postulant whose eyes were so inflamed that the doctor ordered her to be kept in total darkness for several weeks. The solace of reading, drawing, painting or embroidery was, of course, denied her and Mother Aikenhead was sorely puzzled by the problem of what to do to cheer the lonely little soul. Then an idea struck her. The postulant was musical. A guitar would be just the thing! So the long dark hours were lightened by the kindly thought of the Rev. Mother. The postulant, Miss Clifford, recovered to become Sister Mary Lucy, and in due season Mistress of Novices and one of Mother Aikenhead's greatest friends. The guitar was looked upon as a noviceship heirloom. Many a time in later years it was produced at recreation time and the skilful fingers of Mother Mary Lucy accompanied the fresh young voices in their song.

Her kindness of heart shone forth engagingly in the correction of her religious children. She could be severe when occasion demanded, but towards those whose faults were not deliberate she was gentleness itself.

A novice who was once serving at table, without, as she herself said later, being " very well up in the business," had to carry a dish from the kitchen to the refectory. It was large and heavy; the distance seemed not to lessen but to grow; muscles got weaker and weaker until at last they surrendered, and with a sickening thud the dish went crashing to the floor. The joint of mutton slithered along runways of white sauce; the satellite turnips scampered exultingly north and south, in a new found independence. The novice turned and fled!

When the story reached Mother Aikenhead she asked that the delinquent be brought to her. Along came the novice, dejected, humiliated, her eyes red with tears, convinced that her father would soon be in the parlour downstairs and that her trunk would have to be packed, ready for departure.

She was met, on the contrary, with open arms. " Oh, my poor child!" came Rev. Mother's sweet voice, " what happened you? They gave you too large a dish to carry. Are you hurt?"

" No, Rev. Mother, but I broke the dish and let the mutton fall all over the floor."

" Well, my child, and what of that? If the mutton wouldn't go to them, let them go to the mutton! Come, sit here beside me. Now drink this glass of lemonade and forget all about it."

Mother Aikenhead was happiest when surrounded by the novices. One of her favourite " excursions " was a journey round the garden in her bath chair, which they came in turn to push. One day an accident happened. A novice taking a corner too sharply, caused the chair to overbalance, and the invalid, who could do nothing to break her fall, shot face downwards on to the gravel. There she lay, unable to move. A horrified silence descended on the group; and the air was rent with a cry: " I've killed her. I've killed her! She's dead."

" No, I'm not," came the emphatic reply, " but you're not going to leave me here, are you?" For so paralysed were the novices that no one moved to pick her up! They got her somehow back into the chair. The dragging and pulling she endured in the process must have been torture to one who was never out of pain. On the way into the house, however, she gave no sign of any ill effects. Her one anxiety was for the novice, whose cheeks were still as white as her veil.

Nobody was quicker than the Rev. Mother to see what was wanting in an act of virtue. One morning Sister Mary Ambrose, who had charge of the housekeeping, came to her room to report a breakage.

" Rev. Mother," she said, " the wind blew a gale last night and when I came to the store-room I found the two Cork crockery-pans in pieces on the floor. I left them on the windows and the wind blew them in."

"My heart," said Mother Aikenhead, "come here. Where is the humility of a Sister of Charity? Are you trying to put the fault on Almighty God? You know well that the articles were valuable and that you ought to have placed them on the floor. Sister," she added, half in earnest, half in jest, "you are as much use to me as that chair. Indeed not quite so much, for the chair holds my clothes without destroying them. Now be off!"

But it was not the novices and young Sisters alone whom the Rev. Mother had to correct. Sometimes she had to call Mary Aikenhead to account, for her temper at times was hasty. There were moments when she acted not merely promptly but impetuously. Those who had known her in the early days, when she was gentle almost to the point of timidity, observed the change with some surprise. They attributed it rightly to the acute spinal irritation from which she habitually suffered and to the severity of the remedies prescribed.

She herself was well aware of this weakness and was the first to see her error when she had rushed to a conclusion or given an unnecessary reprimand. She would make amends then in the most touching manner for the impatient word. It cost her constant attention and effort to overcome this fault but she succeeded and with advancing age the gentleness, so characteristic of her in youth, returned.

No matter how busy Mother Aikenhead might be, or how engrossing the correspondence in which she was engaged, she was ready to welcome anyone who came or was sent to her. It might be the Archbishop himself; it might be her "dearest Anna Maria"; it might be a doctor from St. Vincent's; it might be a poor man looking for work. They belonged in her eyes, one and all, to the family of Christ and were graciously received as coming from Him. When the portress, Sister Mary Monica, tapped on her door with the news that someone wished to see her, she laid the pen aside and, if unable to go downstairs, told the Sister to bring the visitor up.

Dandy, of doubtful parentage, of no great beauty, but with a faithful doggy heart, and Sister Mary Monica were her two great friends. When Dandy was not with Rev. Mother he was sure to be in the little room off the hall where Sister was accustomed to sew while attending to the door. At the first tinkle of the bell he would rush to the mat and stand there, ears cocked, tail erect, his whole attitude tense with expectation. If the caller was someone he knew, his short, sharp barks of delight would convey to Mother Aikenhead the information that a friend had arrived. A stranger, on the other hand, was sniffed at and surrounded and treated as a suspect with rumbling growls until Sister Mary Monica gave the "All's well." Thereupon Dandy would bury the hatchet and be pleased to co-operate; indeed he would lead the way upstairs himself and trot into the room with a knowing air, as much as to say, "Here we are!"

Mother Aikenhead's room was square, fairly large, though not very lofty, on the second storey to the right of the hall door. Two windows, broad rather than high, gave a view on to the green, tree-shaded lawn, while a third, on the west side, afforded a glimpse of the garden, where flowers, fruit and vegetables flourished. Great oak folding doors extended from wall to wall, filling the space opposite the front windows and forming a background to the Rev. Mother's figure as she sat at a circular, green-covered table. On this stood her writing desk and on it, too, were piled books, papers and letters. To the left, above the fireplace, hung a large oil painting of an old hermit lost in meditation. A book lay open on his knee; one hand closed peacefully on the other; the chasm between heaven and earth was bridged and the spiritual atmosphere of the room heightened imperceptibly by this presence.

A hundred years have passed and still the hermit ponders. The room has remained almost unaltered since Mother Aikenhead's death. Close to the window through which she so often gazed in prayerful wonder at the glory of the setting sun is the chair in which she sat. Near by is her writing desk, with its quill pen and old-fashioned inkstand. The books she read and loved lie as if waiting to be opened by her busy hand. The invalid chair, which for long was regarded as part of herself, stands in its corner motionless. So unchanged is the room that on knocking at the door one would hardly be surprised to be greeted by the friendly bark of a little black dog or to hear a deep motherly voice utter the words: "Well, my heart, and what is the trouble now?"

CHAPTER XIX

Urged on by Love

.T was on a russet September day in the year 1817 while the Congrega-
ion was as yet in its infancy that four words were spoken which will
ive forever enshrined in the hearts of Mother Aikenhead's children.

The occasion was a Clothing Ceremony in North William Street,
o which, at Dr. Murray's request, visitors were admitted for the first
ime. Father Peter Kenney, S.J., was the speaker; the words were
hose which Father Kenney had chosen for his text: *Caritas Christi*
rget nos.

The appeal of the sermon preached that morning lay in its very
implicity. Its central idea was love; the love of God for all His
reatures, their return of love to Him, shown in the case of a Sister
f Charity by her self-sacrificing life of service to the poor. Love,
herefore, was to be the impelling principle and motive force of all
er work. *Caritas Christi urget nos*—the love of Christ drives
s onward. Thus said St. Paul; thus every Sister of Charity would
ay of herself, through the generations, as long as the Congregation
o which she belonged would last.

For Mother Aikenhead was so taken with this idea that she
dopted the text as a motto for herself and her daughters, knowing
hat if the love of Christ once possessed the soul its urge to apostolic
abour would be irresistible. It was so in her own case, for in these
vords lay the inspiration of her projects, the mainspring of her
ctivity. Loving God as intensely as she did she had of necessity to
ove the souls that cost Him the last drop of His blood on Calvary.
'his accounts for her extraordinary zeal for their salvation, a zeal
ourished by prayer and expressing itself incessantly in work.

Nothing emerges more clearly from her correspondence than her
aith in prayer. In great things and in small it was her one resource.
he was always begging the prayers of others. Her letters, she once
aid, were like litanies, for "pray, pray," came at the end of every

sentence, while many a paragraph was rounded off with a significant "Amen," her constant aspiration, a word that concentrated within itself all the holy desires of her heart. In its use she felt that she was chiming in with the prayers and praises of all the angels and friends of God in heaven and on earth.

"Amen. Often, my child, say that holy word fervently and pray it for me as often as you can," was one of the little requests frequently made to her children. Her own prayers were unceasing. During the age-long hours of pain, when her soul was being purified and her body wasting away like a grain of incense in the thurible, the fragrant perfume of her prayer ascended before the throne of God.

The thought of its being "a glorious lot to live and labour for God" was a ruling idea in Mother Aikenhead's mind, and so it is not surprising to find her with a high esteem for manual work, so sanctified by Our Divine Lord's thirty years of humble, hidden toil. She herself was most industrious. When she first became ill, at the early age of forty-four, and it seemed as though her active life were over, she smilingly remarked that if God was taking away the use of her feet she still had her hands—and a fine, capable pair they proved themselves to be, never for a moment idle.

During the months prior to the opening of St. Vincent's Hospital, when her spinal trouble was very acute, she hemmed thirty pairs of sheets with their accompaniment of pillow and bolster slips, thus forming the nucleus of the future linen store. In course of time she came to take upon herself a multitude of what are called "odd jobs." All sorts of little tasks that would ease the work of the Sisters visiting the poor found their way to her bedside to be carried through by her willing fingers. Altar cloths to be mended, bundles of second-hand clothing to be patched, fancy work for a bazaar in aid of one of her institutions, envelopes to be turned. Many and varied were these occupations.

As she could no longer serve the poor directly and have personal contact with them her only way of exercising her zeal was by helping those who were fortunate enough to be employed in what she regarded as "the most divine of all divine works: to co-operate with God in the salvation of souls."

The "poor lame pen," too, was frequently used in their service, especially in the appeals for funds to keep the missions going, for in none of her houses was the wolf ever far from the door. On Christmas

:ve, 1836, she folded and directed three thousand five hundred
egging letters. They brought her in the magnificent sum of £35!
another time she mentions that four thousand appeals had been
espatched. Typewriters, duplicators and other such labour-saving
evices were not then available. Bread had to be earned by the sweat
f one's brow—in her case by the tireless use of her pen.

In 1833, when a Commission was set up to inquire into the state
f the Irish poor, Mother Aikenhead received a list of queries on the
ıbject. It was a request after her own heart and the letter in reply
'as well worthy of being preserved, so clear a light did it throw on
ıe pitiable conditions that existed in the days when there were no
ɔcial welfare schemes for the Catholic poor. She wrote particularly
bout the district around Sandymount, where she had first-hand in-
ɔrmation from the Sisters working on the sick mission. She told of
ıe widespread unemployment and of the resultant poverty; of the
awning of furniture and tattered bedclothes to obtain food; of many
:ople who had but one insufficient meal in forty-eight hours; of
ımilies numbering as many as eight persons whose only nourish-
ıent was three pints of broth in two days. Twenty of these families
'ere kept from actual starvation by the slender resources of the
ɔnvent. All were in such terrible destitution that to find the most
:serving cases caused difficulty. "Excessive poverty," she continues,
produces a want of cleanliness which aggravates misery. The lanes
ıd streets are filled with filth in Ringsend and Irishtown; there are
ɔ sewers; no attention is paid to the ventilation of the houses, and
ıe poor are obliged to buy even the water they drink; it is of the
orst description and tends to promote disease by its scarcity as by
s quality. The poor have no bedclothes; we have often seen them
:pire on dirty straw and are frequently obliged to furnish them
ith covering before we can approach to administer to their
ants. . . ."

It was a letter so sincere in tone, so graphic in its description, that
must have made the worthy gentlemen of the Commission wince;
t there is no record of Mother Aikenhead's having ever received
ı acknowledgment. Probably it met with the same fate as many
ıother answer to official inquiries; it was marked "Read," filed
vay carefully and left to moulder into dust in some long-forgotten
ɔx.

The way of helping the poor which best pleased Mother Aikenhead was by giving employment. That a man should earn his own livelihood and be responsible for the support of his wife and family was, in her opinion, much more befitting the dignity of a creature of God than that he should depend on the charity of others. It was interesting to see her often counting with satisfaction the number of men employed at one of her convents where building was in progress, as though she were to receive a bonus for each one instead of being hard put to it to pay their wages at the week's end.

" God's providence is assuredly a rich bank," she would confidently say when asked how she managed. But at the same time she would add: " We must do our little best. . . . Our Lord required the Apostles to produce the five loaves and two fishes upon which to work the miracle." She never worried and the men were never left unpaid.

Her anxiety extended beyond the men themselves to their home surroundings, and especially to their children. Through her advice and help many a young lad was put to a trade, while many a young girl was brought to Stanhope Street, trained thoroughly in domesti duties and prepared to face the future worthily as a good wife an mother.

Though her Congregation had been founded primarily to help th poor of Ireland there was nothing narrow or insular about Mothe Aikenhead's sympathies. When Dr. Ullathorne sent her a pamphle giving a harrowing description of convict life in Australia an begging for help, the thought of so many souls in grave danger o being lost touched her apostolic spirit to its depths. She sent a cop of the pamphlet to all her houses with a request for volunteers fo the Australian Mission, though at the time the numbers at home wer small and all were needed. No sacrifice could be too great when s much was at stake. In the same spirit the foundation in Englan was attempted, though it was only after her death that her daughte succeeded in establishing convents there and carrying on their wor amongst the poor.

Zealous as she was to promote the Kingdom of God, she was alwa on her guard lest a false zeal for their own particular works shoul creep imperceptibly into the hearts of her nuns. She wished them be noble-minded enough to rejoice when other Orders were called labour for the glory of God and the good of Ireland. What did matter who did God's work provided it was done? Once when son steps were being taken that seemed to favour the Sisters of Mercy at the expense of her own Congregation she said: "If this be all ordained by Our Heavenly Father for His own glory our hearts ought to utter a fervent 'Amen', even if their advance were to be actually our depression. But in the Holy Church there is room for all."

Great was her love for Ireland. In one sense it is true to say that the Irish poor owe more to her than to any other one person, for it was she who took down the cloister's grill placed it on the hearts of her nuns and sent them to the homes of the poor, to prisons, to build orphanages and hospitals, to gather into happy folds the strayed sheep. She herself was the first nun to go out on the highways and byeways for Christ, to spend herself in wanderings and journeys like St. Paul. Her work was a comforting little candle shedding warm rays of light in the spiritual darkness of the Irish poor.

> "It was a spark from Heaven that lit the flame
> That burns towards the Source from whence it came."

Thanks be to God that light has never grown dim.

St. Mary Magdalen's, Donnybrook, Dublin.

CHAPTER XX

The Lonely Road

"FASTER, MAN, faster!" shouted Doctor O'Ferrall with his head out of the carriage window. "For God's sake hurry!"

"Yessir, yessir," answered the coachman, cracking his whip and urging the horses to greater effort. The doctor sat back in his corner, silent and moody. Outside night had fallen but the darkness was not oppressive, for the air was sweet with the softness of spring. It was not until they swung round from St. Stephen's Green into Harcourt Street that the apothecary ventured to remark: "You haven't very much hope, Sir?"

"No," came the brief response. Then he added: "There's just one chance in a hundred and I'm going to take it. Sir Philip Crampton and Sir Henry Marsh saw her with me this morning; they didn't think she'd last the day and consider it useless our going there to-night. Sir Philip, in fact, said——." He stopped short, not wishing to repeat the surgeon-general's words, which were: "You may do as you like, O'Ferrall; the woman is as dead as if you shot her through the head."

It was almost midnight when they reached Our Lady's Mount. "Thank God you have come," whispered Sister Mary Monica, who was waiting for them in the hall. "Down, Dandy! Quiet, boy!" as the little dog, half-stupefied with sleep, blinked enquiringly at the dark shadows moving up the stairs.

Outside, the coachman wrapped himself in a blanket and settled down for a nap; within, behind the large oak doors of the sitting-room, in the flickering candlelight Dr. O'Ferrall applied himself to what appeared to be the hopeless task of saving Mother Aikenhead's life.

His success was remarkable. Before Lent was over the Rev. Mother was sitting up and her pen was active once more. That was in 1847.

She lived for another eleven years! But by 1858 even Dr. O'Ferrall had to admit that her life's journey was nearing its close. Her work was done. She had accomplished what she had set out to do. Her convents were firmly established; if the branches were as yet small and few the roots were deeply set. As far back as 1833 when the Constitutions drawn up so carefully by Father St. Leger were confirmed by Pope Gregory XVI, she had the joy of knowing that her Congregation was approved by the Church.

The signing of the deeds relating to the transfer of Benada Abbey to the nuns was her last official act. Her pen, which had rendered such faithful service to the poor and to her own religious family, was laid aside now, never to be used again.

For the last six months of her life her sufferings were severe and continuous, as her heart by then had been grievously affected. Now signs of dropsy began to appear. In addition there were painful attacks of rheumatism, while bronchitis rendered her breathing so difficult that she could no longer lie down. When paralysis attacked the muscles at the back of her neck they were unable to support her head. It fell forward painfully on her chest. A Sister had to stand behind her and hold it up when she wished to take food. Her twenty-seven years of illness culminated thus in intense torture. The infirmarians, and even Dr. O'Ferrall, who loved her as a mother, were moved to tears at the sight of constant agony which they were powerless to relieve.

Never did she utter a word of complaint. Sister Mary Monica asserted that she had never even seen a frown on her face. One morning when Sister Mary Camillus asked her: "How did you pass the night, Mother?" her simple reply, "On the Cross with Our Lord," revealed the secret of her amazing patience, the union of her pains with His. Not only was she being given a share in His physical sufferings but she was also allowed to taste something of the abandonment and desolation of Calvary that wrung from His dying lips the cry: "My God, my God, why hast Thou forsaken Me?"

One by one death had claimed those treasured friends who from the beginning had been her fellow workers. Dr. Murray, Fr. St. Leger, Fr. Kenney and Mother Catherine—all were gone, and Mother Aikenhead experienced to the full the loneliness of one who finds herself the last of her generation. Far more trying, however, was the dereliction of spirit with which it pleased God to afflict her at the end. Oppressed with an intense feeling of her own unworthiness she was often heard to cry aloud to God for mercy, for pity, for pardon. Her loving intimacy with Him appeared to have vanished. Most distressing of all, Holy Communion, which throughout her life had been her solace and support, was now a cause of terror. No one understood her state of soul or could offer consolation, till after several months of darkness God Himself chose to lift the cloud of spiritual anguish by sending a Dominican Father to guide her along the last weary stretch of road. Under his skilful direction the soft radiance of God's kindly light returned and flooded her soul once again.

When it became known that the end was near and that there was no longer hope of even a partial recovery, Mother Aikenhead had many visits from her own daughters. Everyone wished to say farewell to her. Not only did they come from the Dublin houses but from Cork, Waterford, Clonmel and Clarinbridge, all anxious to receive her blessing and a parting word of advice to be treasured while they lived.

One visitor, however, was sternly refused admittance. Sister Mary Monica had rigid ideas about the decorum becoming in a sickroom. It was, she thought, no place for a dog, so for a long time all poor Dandy's efforts to see his mistress came to naught. One evening when Mother Aikenhead was easier than she had been for several days she prevailed on the zealous infirmarian to go to Benediction instead of remaining with her, as had become her custom. Hardly had Sister's footsteps died away than slowly and stiffly the little black dog began the ascent of the stairs. Age was telling on him, too; he was blind in one eye and scant of breath, but his faithful doggy heart was unchanged. As he nosed his way into the cell everything was very quiet. Mother Aikenhead was lying with her eyes closed, the brown beads slipping through her fingers. He padded softly over to the bed. She heard him and whispered joyfully: " Oh, Dandy, my poor boy, you've come to see me!"

" Yes, yes, yes," wagged his tail, " and I'd come every day if only they'd let me," as he stood with his forepaws on the bed and with his pink tongue gently caressed her hand. It was a happy reunion. He listened to the dear voice until she said: " Down, boy, down to your box." Ever obedient (not for nothing was he a convent dog), he turned away and was safely below stairs when the Sisters emerged from the chapel. The Reverend Mother smiled as she took up her beads once more. How clever of the little animal to have outwitted Sister! Then her eye fell on the sheet and her laughter turned to dismay, for there, on the snowy surface, lay the imprint of two dusty paws!

As the hot summer days crept slowly by there was little change in her condition save that she was growing weaker. Little by little the veil behind which God hides Himself had been worn thinner, until He shone as clear to the eyes of her soul as a sunbeam through a cobweb. She awaited in peace the final call.

The evening before she died Sister Mary Camillus reported that the nuns in Donnybrook had sent their messenger to enquire for her. This was a woman who was often employed on errands by the Sisters and was, therefore, well known to Mother Aikenhead. On hearing that Katie was in the house the dying nun said slowly, for speech was already difficult, "I think she needs a new pair of boots; won't you get them for her?" Then followed a pause so long that Sister Mary Camillus, thinking she was dozing off, was about to leave the room. But she spoke again. She had recalled that St. Mary Magdalen's Day was a special feast for the penitents. "If I die to-morrow"—the feeble voice was scarcely above a whisper—"if I die to-morrow do not tell the poor penitents until the day after, as it would spoil their pleasure."

These were to be her last recorded words. It will be agreed that they closed fittingly a life of practical charity and thought for others.

At noon the following day, July 22nd, 1858, she received Holy Viaticum, food for her journey to eternity. Gradually then she began to slip away from the world of earth. When she could no longer see the faces of her children gathered about her bed she could distinguish their voices as they prayed. "Holy Mary, Mother of God, pray for us sinners now and at the hour of our death. Amen." The hour of her death had come at last. She had seen so many others go before; now it was her own turn, and the journey, as always, had to be made alone.

"My Jesus, mercy!" her lips tried to frame the words but no sound would come. The voices around her grew fainter till they were like the murmur of waves on a distant shore. Then they ceased altogether. An icy coldness was spreading slowly over her body. It reached her heart, bringing with it for a moment human fear.

Suddenly she became aware that close by was Someone dear and familiar, Someone Whose presence made all dread and uncertainty take flight as shadows before the rising sun. The road was no longer lonely, and in joy she passed along it to its end.

Foreign Missions.

CHAPTER XXI

The Light that Shines

Footsteps up and down, up and down! All day long they came and went. Boots crunching on the gravel or creaking clumsily in an effort to tiptoe in the chapel mingled with the lighter tread of the women, while the soft pit-pat of barefoot boys and girls, the rattle of rosary beads, the whisper of prayers and sighs of grief filled the air with a muffled confusion of sound.

From far and near they came, the poor of Dublin, to mourn the loss of her who had been their friend and more than their friend—their mother. They thronged about her coffin, sprinkled her generously with holy water and curiously eyed the piece of paper held in her waxen fingers, speculating in undertones as to what it meant. Yellow with age, the ink faded, it was a copy of the vows made on that day some forty-three years before when Mary Frances Aikenhead became the Bride of Christ and the candle of her life's work was lit.

Towards evening a group of labouring men came to the hall door asking to see the " head nun." For them there was only one Rev. Mother and they had already paid their last respects to her. They had a request to make, one out of the ordinary, too, and so, with the awkwardness common to their kind, in the presence of Mother Francis Magdalen, they shuffled and nudged and could get nothing coherent into their sentences. Then one of them, a fine young fellow in the middle twenties, with a shock of dark hair and honest blue eyes, took a grip of himself and stepped forward. His name was Danny O'Connell and he had once been held in Mother Aikenhead's arms as a small patient in St. Vincent's Hospital. He explained what it was they wanted, the honour of bearing the coffin to the grave. " She always done what she could for us, and we want to do what we can for her," he ended, while his comrades regarded the nun hopefully.

Mother Francis Magdalen was deeply touched. " It is a very kind thought, Danny," she replied, "and we greatly appreciate it, but you understand that I cannot give you permission without consulting the other Sisters. It is a most unusual case. If it were a political leader such an action would be quite fitting, but——"

"Yerrah, ma'am," interposed a grand old workman, "she," jerking his head in the direction of the chapel, "she's done more for us than an army of other people, God rest her soul!" and a chorus of hearty "Amens" followed Mother Francis Magdalen from the parlour.

She was quite undecided till Sister Mary Camillus, in answer to the argument that it was outside the established order of things, said quietly, and with just the glimmer of a smile behind the sad brown eyes: "Don't refuse them! All her life poor Rev. Mother listened to those words, 'It's never been done before,' and you know the answer she always gave, 'That's no reason why it shouldn't be done now'!"

And just as "Little Miss Mary" half a century earlier was carried to the chapel on Daddy John's shoulders so was the first Superior General of the Sisters of Charity borne on the shoulders of Dublin working-men to her last resting-place. From Harold's Cross the funeral procession slowly wound its way by Leinster Road to Rathmines, thence to Ranelagh. Up Sandford Road it went, turning to the left down Belmont Avenue and into Donnybrook, where, in the cemetery within the convent grounds, the rich brown earth was piled above a freshly dug grave.

* * * * * *

Once, during her last illness Mother Aikenhead said: "After my death the Congregation will flourish," and as the years passed the truth of these words was clearly seen. Others took up where she left off, and to-day there are few phases or conditions of human suffering to which the charity of Christ as practised by her daughters, does not extend.

One of the principal works of the Congregation, as in the days of the foundress, is the visitation of the sick poor, and the nuns who spend their lives journeying from street to street, from house to house, up and down dark tenement staircases in search of souls in need of help, are but following in her wake. Like their good Mother they are armed with a "mission bag" and no magic wand ever produced such a variety of articles as comes forth from the depths of this innocent-looking black leather receptacle. From a plug of tobacco for the "old man," or an infallible rub for granny's rheumatism to a layette for the latest arrival; from an ounce of tea, worth its weight in gold during the "ration," to a wedding ring for a marriage ceremony long delayed, there are no limits to its possibilities! Children's faces brighten as Sister's fingers open the precious bag. Is it sweets to-day? Or a pair of shoes for Mary? Or the doll she promised baby? Or the surplice for Paddy, soon to be on the altar? Or . . . ? Or. . . ?

From the sick mission spring numerous spiritual and social activities according to the needs of the age. Amongst these, for example, are sodalities, guilds, the management of week-end retreats, girls' clubs, technical and dramatic classes, hostels for girls, a holiday home for working girls and, of course, the Christmas parties and summer outings for which the convents are famous!

In localities where there is great poverty, food centres are organised where penny dinners can be had. There is a special one for expectant mothers where, for three months before and after the baby's birth they get a nourishing midday meal. Mother Aikenhead would have been in her element here. One can picture her serving out the meals herself, having made sure beforehand that there was plenty of food, piping hot, that the stew was tasty and the pudding sufficiently sweet.

The education and care of children is another important work whose origin goes back to the early days of her religious life with the fourteen little girls in North William Street. Their number has now grown to tens of thousands, what between day schools, orphanages, industrial schools and training schools where older girls learn domestic economy. Most of the schools are under the National Board but there are some which cater for the needs of children capable and desirous of doing a secondary course, but unable to pay the high fees and procure the expensive uniforms required by the normal secondary schools.

St. Vincent's Hospital, Mother Aikenhead's greatest achievement and the foundation closest to her heart, still carries on its work of charity amongst the poor, not merely of Dublin but of almost every part of Ireland. It, too, has outstripped her wildest imaginings, for never could she, dreamer though she was of dreams, have conceived the idea of a 20th century hospital with its up-to-date equipment. It is a far cry from the operations of long ago when surgeons worked in their frock coats and top hats to the brilliantly lit theatres with their tiled walls and floors, the sparkling array of instruments, the sterilisers, the anæsthetics, the masked and white-gowned doctors and nurses. What would she think of the X-Ray Department? Of the Diet Kitchen? Of the Out-patients' Department? No doubt she would think of the parable of the mustard seed and rejoice.

Nor should we forget what may be called the hospital's "appendices," nursing and convalescent homes and hospices for the dying. The first of these was at Harold's Cross, in the convent made sacred to the Sisters by her death. Many others, facing their last few miles along the "lonely road" have been cheered and comforted by the happy atmosphere within its walls. The second, St. Joseph's Hospice for the Dying, Mare Street, Hackney, is said to be the fruit of thirty years' prayer of the late Fr. Peter Gallwey, S.J. It was the dream of his life to see a home in London where those considered ineligible for other hospitals might die in peace, strengthened by all the consolations of religion. The same idea underlay the foundation at Clydebank, Glasgow, of St. Margaret's Hospice. Like Hackney and Harold's Cross, it is in very truth a gateway through which many a strayed sheep has passed to find his way back, at the eleventh hour, to the welcoming arms of the Good Shepherd.

There is a hospital for incurable patients suffering from tuberculosis and cancer, and there are hospitals and convalescent homes especially for children.

The building formerly known as the Children's Hospital, Buckingham Street, was not without historic connections. Originally it was the town house of Alderman John Claudius Beresford, notorious for the cruel zeal with which he helped to crush the rising of '98. Lavish in his hospitality, agreeable in private life, with his Scottish wife and bevy of handsome children, he fitted perfectly into the style of living of his class in the Dublin of that time. It is hard to reconcile the two aspects of his character, the genial host, glass in hand, calling for another song, and the sinister master of the rebel-hunting troops of informers and light cavalry, known as "Beresford's Bloodhounds." Once an unfortunate man was caught, he was brought into the riding-house, suspended from a triangle and flogged till he made his " confession," true or false, or fainted in his agony, while the Alderman stood by and watched. Was it the irony of fate or just common retribution that the descendants of those Croppies so brutally treated should have been nursed back to health under the roof of Beresford's mansion? He and his friends who helped to misrule Ireland during the 18th century are gone, leaving scarce a trace outside the history books, while the memory of an obscure nun, the daughter of a provincial doctor, remains fresh and green with the immortality of good works.

In 1879, on the expiration of the lease, the hospital was removed to its present position in Temple Street.

The youngest patients in Temple Street are only a few hours old. Here again Mother Aikenhead would have cause for joy in all that is being done for the sick and suffering little ones. Not far away, at Cappagh, St. Mary's Open-air Hospital also accomplishes wonders for children requiring orthopædic treatment. Situated amid luxuriant trees and rolling grasslands, Cappagh resounds with the shouts and laughter of the sun-kissed boys and girls, most of whom are on frames or have some part of their little bodies encased in plaster of Paris. As their treatment lasts in many cases for a long period, lessons must not be neglected. In addition to ordinary school work there are classes in needlework, handwork, leatherwork and basket-making. Their fingers, like Mother Aikenhead's, are all the busier because their feet are still.

Another work of a different sort for children is that done by St. Patrick's Guild. From time to time an advertisement in the news-paper will attract attention and make one ask: " What is all this about?"

> " Good Catholic home wanted for little Paul, aged 3½ years, brown eyes, gentle, refined, good-humoured, healthy. No fee. Full surrender . . ."

and so on. The wording will change. It may be curly-headed Peter, blue-eyed Agnes, black-haired Dorothy who wants a mother, but the idea in the background is always the same, the endeavour to get a homeless child adopted. Each tiny, unwanted baby is brought at the age of eight days to St. Patrick's Infant Hospital, Temple Hill, Blackrock, there to be reared till old enough to be given into the care of a foster mother or to be adopted. Occasionally the baby is only left with the nuns for a short period, till the mother is married, when she takes back her child. Unluckily this arrangement is all too rare. Each year between eighty and a hundred of these children find their way to England or America to gladden childless homes by their sweet presence.

Naturally the greatest precautions are taken with regard to the choice of foster parents in Ireland and adoptive parents abroad. Where the child is fully surrendered four people benefit by the arrangement. The unmarried mother, with her child safely and happily provided for, can start life afresh; the baby, wanted and cherished, grows up without the stigma of illegitimacy; and the husband and wife, to whom God has denied the blessing of children, find an outlet for their parental love in the care and upbringing of little Paul, or Peter, or Agnes or Dorothy.

Another work that has a pathetic interest is St. Mary's Home for the Blind, Merrion. From small beginnings it has increased so far as to afford accommodation for nearly two hundred afflicted ones. Visitors are intrigued to see the boys and girls at school, their sensitive fingers doing the work of eyes; or to watch the older girls and women rapidly knitting jumpers with most intricate patterns. If time permits they are sure to be entertained to vocal and instrumental music at which the blind excel. Love of music is the greatest consolation they have. For them it is the blue sea with its white-capped waves, the sunshine dancing on green fields, the trees in autumn, the flitting clouds across the sky at night.

A haven for the aged, those who through the harsh grindings of life have no longer a hearth of their own, is found in St. Monica's Widows' Home, attached to Gardiner Street Convent. Apart from the comfort of the tastefully furnished bedrooms and the appetising cuisine, what strikes the visitor most of all is the " uninstitutional " atmosphere. Yet there are eighty-two old ladies to be cared for. There is great freedom about the place; they come and go as they wish, and if they so desire lie on in the mornings, regardless of whether they are well or ill. Small amenities these may be, but they can make all the difference between an institution and a home.

Mother Aikenhead's love for penitents still finds expression in St. Mary Magdalen's, Donnybrook, and St. Vincent's, Cork. Nor could anything be more in harmony with her spirit than the establishment, through the zeal of her gifted daughter, Mother Mary Arsenius

Morrogh-Bernard, of a woollen mill at Foxford in 1892. Heavy rents, overcrowding, and a notoriously sterile, inhospitable soil combined to make conditions in the village and its neighbourhood well-nigh intolerable. Poverty was a chronic evil which the local resources could never overcome. An industry of some size seemed to be the only remedy. So Mother Mary Arsenius determined that Foxford should have an industry. She was a nun without commercial training, and it was the end of the 19th century, the age of the new industrial order, of grimy factories, huge machines, complicated processes of exchange, sale in distant markets, organisation on a giant scale. What did all that matter? She would do her little part and God would do the rest. " Providence will provide," Mother Arsenius was accustomed to exclaim in every difficulty. In this case Providence did provide. A Protestant millowner from County Tyrone, became her good friend and technical adviser. The Mother General mortgaged the chief house of the Congregation to secure the necessary capital. Machinery was bought and on April 26th, 1892, the sluice gates of the Moy were opened and the factory that had been given the name " Providence Woollen Mills " began to function. The poor were enabled to earn their daily bread and at the same time given the opportunity of becoming worthy citizens of the City of God, for in Foxford, the material and the spiritual were always to go hand in hand. The mill has had its ups and downs, its strains and stresses, its heavy debts, its bad seasons, but under the all-seeing eye of Providence it has in general prospered since that raw April morning in the nineties of the last century.

The Congregation in Australia has advanced by leaps and bounds, and throughout New South Wales, Victoria, Tasmania and Queensland the successors of those five pioneer nuns, who so bravely set their hands to the plough, continue to labour. Hospitals, nursing homes, hospices for the dying, parochial and high schools, colleges, orphanages, the visitation of the poor—the same works are carried on as in Ireland, England and Scotland, in the same spirit of *Caritas Christi urget nos*. There is just one difference, however. In the early days of this mission field communication between Dublin and Parramatta was so difficult—it took months for letters to travel to and from Ireland—that it was thought advisable to make the Australian branch of the Congregation self-governing, so Mother Mary John was appointed the first Superior General in New South Wales.

To-day the Mother House and Novitiate are at Potts Point, Sydney, but the bond of charity scorns distance and the Irish and Australian daughters of Mother Aikenhead continue to live one in heart and soul, inspired with the same zeal for God's poor, united in loyalty to the ideals and aspirations of their holy Foundress.

On the last day of September, 1948, one hundred and ten years after Mother Mary John and her companions set foot on Australian soil, a twenty-five thousand ton liner, the *Athlone Castle,* raised anchor at Southampton and steamed for the Dark Continent. On board were three Sisters of Charity who had responded to the call of the poor of Christ in Africa. Their sphere of labour would henceforth be among the Batonga people, and at Chikuni, Northern Rhodesia, their new convent home would lie, one hundred and fifty miles from civilisation. There, in due course, other Sisters would come to join them.

This mission, now under the care of the Irish Jesuit Fathers, extends over a wide area, for round the flourishing mission centre are between forty and fifty villages in outlying districts. The spiritual welfare of all this area is the responsibility of the Jesuit priests. In Africa, as at home, nursing plays a large part in the work of the nuns, but whether it is the sick or ailing in dispensary or hospital, the mothers and babies, or the poor lepers with their corrupting bodies that call forth their charity, it is Christ Himself in the persons of these His little ones upon whom their care is lavished. And the Sisters, too, teaching in school or training college see His image reflected in the gleaming dark eyes turned eagerly up to theirs. It is service to Him and the continuation of His redemptive work to make those, His black-skinned children, white-souled temples of the Holy Ghost.

Lastly there is the Mother House, which in 1879 was transferred from Harold's Cross to Mount St. Anne's, Milltown. Here resides the Mother General, in whose hands, under God, lies the guardianship of the Congregation. Here also are the novices, on whose young shoulders will rest the responsibility of keeping alive in the future the little flame which their Mother lit, and which, it is hoped, the spirit that animated her, the love of Christ and of Christ's poor, will keep alight for ever.

In September, 1953, a Foundation was made at Los Angeles, California, at the request of His Eminence Cardinal McIntyre.

Bibliography

ATKINSON, SARAH. *Mary Aikenhead, Her Life, Her Work and Her Friends.* Dublin, 1879.

ATKINSON, SARAH. *Essays.* Dublin, 1895.

BELLOC, B. R. *Historic Nuns.* London, 1898.

BURKE-SAVAGE, R., S.J. *Catherine McAuley.* Dublin, 1949.

CULLEN, REV. JOHN H. *The Australian Daughters of Mary Aikenhead.* Sydney, 1938.

GIBBONS, MARGARET. *The Life of Margaret Aylward.* London, 1928.

MEMBER OF THE CONGREGATION. *The Life and Work of Mary Aikenhead.* London, 1925.

ULLATHORNE, ARCHBISHOP. *Autobiography.* London, 1891.

WIDDES, J. D. H. *An Account of the Schools of Surgery, Royal College of Surgeons, Dublin.* Edinburgh, 1948.

WODSWORTH. W. D. *A History of the Ancient Foundling Hospital of Dublin,* 1876.

Contemporary Newspapers. Dublin Historical Record.

The Gentlemen's and Citizens' Almanack.

HOUSES OF THE CONGREGATION AND INSTITUTIONS UNDER THE CARE OF THE SISTERS OF CHARITY.*

IRELAND.

Mount St. Anne's, Milltown, Dublin.
Mother House of the Congregation.
Novitiate.
National School.

Convent of the Purification, Stanhope Street, Dublin.
To which is attached:
St. Mary's Training School for Girls.
National School.

Convent of the Assumption, Gardiner Street, Dublin.
National School.
Prenatal Dining Centre.
Evening Club for Girls.
St. Monica's Widows' Home is attached to this convent.

Convent of the Nativity of Our Lady, Sandymount, Dublin.
Industrial School and National School.

St. Mary Magdalen's Asylum, Donnybrook, Dublin.

St. Vincent's Hospital, St. Stephen's Green, Dublin.

Our Lady's Mount, Harold's Cross, Dublin.
Hospice for the Dying.
National School.

St. Mary's Home for the Blind, Merrion, Dublin.
To which is attached:
St. Gerard's Convalescent Home for Children.

St. Joseph's Orphanage, Mountjoy Street, Dublin.
To which is attached:
St. Mary's Convent Schools, King's Inns Street.
The Josephian National School.
St. Joseph's Intermediate School.

The Children's Hospital, Temple Street, Dublin.
To which is attached:
The "Anthonian Press". The monthly magazine, *St. Anthony's Annals.*

Convent of St. Laurence O'Toole, Seville Place, Dublin.
National School.
Food Centre (Penny Dinners).
Attached to this convent are
Hostels for nuns, business girls and working girls out of employment.
The Little Flower Monthly is published from this convent.

Convent of Our Lady of Good Counsel, Basin Lane, Dublin.
National Schools.

*Sick Mission and Sodalities attached to practically all the Houses.

Convent of St. Agnes, Crumlin, Dublin.
National Schools.
Prenatal Dining Centre.
Evening Club for Girls.

St. Mary's Orthopædic Hospital, Cappagh, Finglas, Co. Dublin.

Convent of the Visitation, Baldoyle, Co. Dublin.
Auxiliary Orthopædic Hospital.

Convalescent Home, Linden, Blackrock, Co. Dublin.

St. Patrick's Infant Hospital, Temple Hill, Blackrock, Co. Dublin.
Rescue Work.
Arrangements for adoptions carried out at St. Patrick's Guild, 50 Middle Abbey Street, Dublin.

Stella Maris, Baily, Co. Dublin.
Sick Mission and Sodalities.

Convent of the Holy Family, Bray, Co. Wicklow.
To which is attached:
Holiday Home for Girls.
House of Retreats.
National School.

St. Vincent's Convent, St. Mary's Road, Cork.
Magdalen Asylum.
National Schools.

St. Patrick's Hospital, Wellington Road, Cork.
Hospital for Incurable Diseases.

St. Helen's Convent, Blarney, Co. Cork.
Sisters conduct dispensary for Mill Workers.

Convent of Our Lady of Charity. Lady Lane, Waterford.
To which is attached:
Training School for Girls.
National School.

Star of the Sea, Tramore, Co. Waterford.
National School.

St. Joseph's Girls' Industrial School, Kilkenny.

St. Patrick's Boys' Industrial School, Kilkenny.

Convent of Our Lady of the Angels, Clonmel, Co. Tipperary.
To which is attached:
St. Michael's Training School for Girls.
National School.

Convent of Our Lady of Mercy, Clarinbridge, Co. Galway.
National School.

Convent of Our Lady of Benada, Co. Sligo.
Industrial School and National School.

Convent of the Sacred Heart, Ballaghaderreen, Co. Roscommon.
Industrial School and National School.

Convent of Divine Providence, Foxford, Co. Mayo.
Providence Woollen Mills.
National School.
Music School.

ENGLAND.

St. Joseph's Hospice for the Dying, Mare Street, Hackney, London.
St. Brigid's Hostel for Business Girls, Hammersmith, London.
St. Mary's residential School for Girls, Walthamstow, London.
Sisters teach in the local Elementary and Secondary Schools.
St. Margaret's, Rockferry, Cheshire.
To which is attached:
House of Retreats.
Home for Old Ladies.
Hostel for Business Girls.
St. Elizabeth's Convent, Claughton Road, Birkenhead, Cheshire.
Sick Mission, Sodalities and clubs conducted in five parishes.
Mother and Child Clinic attached to convent.
St. Anne's Convent, Saltley, Birmingham.
Sisters teach in the local Elementary and Secondary Schools.
St. Catherine's Convent, Oldfield Road, Bath.
Nursing Home.
Convent of the Holy Ghost, Basingstoke, Hants.
Private School.
Convent of Our Lady of Lourdes, Knowle, Bristol.
Sisters teach in local Elementary School.
Convent of the Sacred Heart, Sowerby Bridge, Halifax, Yorkshire.
Junior School.

SCOTLAND.

St. Margaret's Hospice for the Dying, Millbrae Crescent, Clydebank, Glasgow.
Sisters teach in Primary and Junior Secondary Departments of local School.

AFRICA.

Convent of the Immaculate Heart of Mary, Chikuni, Chisekesi Siding, North Rhodesia.
School.
Dispensary.
Hospital.

AMERICA.

Convent of the Guardian Angels, Long Beach, California, U.S.A.
Junior School.

LIST OF CONVENTS, SCHOOLS AND INSTITUTIONS OF THE CONGREGATION OF THE SISTERS OF CHARITY IN AUSTRALIA

EW SOUTH WALES.

t. Vincent's Convent, Potts Point, Sydney.
Mother House of the Congregation.

Attached to it are:

Bethania, the Novitiate House.
St. Vincent's College for boarders and day pupils.
St. Mary's Cathedral School, Intermediate and Commercial Courses.
Sacred Heart Parochial School, Darlinghurst.
St. Canice's Parochial School.

t. Vincent's Hospital, Sydney.

t. Mary's Convent, Liverpool.
Intermediate Day and Boarding School.
Parochial School, Cabramatta, is staffed from this convent.

Ionte Oliveto Convent, Woollahra.
High School and St. Joseph's Parochial School.

ethlehem Convent, Ashfield.
College and Parochial School.

t. Mary's Convent, Hurstville.
Parochial Schools.
South Hurstville Primary School.

St. Anne's Orphanage, Liverpool.

acred Heart Hospice, Darlinghurst, Sydney.

t. Joseph's Hospital, Auburn.
Attached to this convent is:
St. John's Parochial School.

t. Francis Xavier's Convent, Concord.
Parochial School.
Primary School at Mortlake attached to this convent.

Iount St. Mary's, Katoomba, Blue Mountains.
College for boarders and day pupils.
Parochial School.

Iount St. Patrick's, Paddington.
Intermediate High School and Parochial School.

t. Vincent's Hospital, Lismore.
Attached to this is:
St. Joseph's Hospice for the Dying.

t. Vincent's Hospital, Bathurst.

St. Thomas' Convent, Lewisham.
Intermediate Parochial School.

St. Ambrose's Convent, Concord West.
Parochial School.

VICTORIA.

Our Lady of the Sacred Heart, Grey Street, East Melbourne.
Catholic Ladies' College and three Parochial Schools:—
St. John's, East Melbourne.
St. George's, Carlton.
St. Joseph's, Collingwood.

St. John's Convent, Clifton Hill.
Parochial School.

St. Columba's Convent, Essendon.
A College is attached to this convent and the Sisters also conduct:—
St. Monica's Parochial School, Essendon.
St. Teresa's, North Essendon.
St. Vincent's, North Essendon.

St. Vincent's Hospital, Fitzroy, Melbourne.
Attached to the Hospital is St. Vincent's Maternity Home.

Mount St. Evin's Private Hospital, Fitzroy, Melbourne.

"Caritas Christi" Hospice for the Dying Poor, Kew.

TASMANIA.

St. Joseph's Convent, Hobart.
St. Joseph's Parochial School.
St. Luke's Primary School.

St. Joseph's Orphanage, Hobart.

Mount Carmel Primary School, Sandy Bay, Hobart.

St. Vincent's Hospital, Launceston.

QUEENSLAND.

St. Vincent's Hospital, Toowoomba.

St. Finbarr's Convent, Ashgrove.
Parochial School and High School.

Index